STEWART

STEWART

FORMULA 1 RACING TEAM

David Tremayne

Haynes Publishing

DEDICATION

To the driver of car No 5, whose
efforts to wrestle a decent performance
out of it at Silverstone in 1967 were
frustrated on the day, yet ignited a
lifelong passion in a 14-year-old boy.

© David Tremayne 1999

First published in November 1999

A catalogue record for this book is
available from the British Library

ISBN: 1 85960 423 4

Library of Congress catalog card no. 99-73261

Haynes North America Inc.,
861 Lawrence Drive, Newbury Park,
California 91320, USA.

Published by Haynes Publishing, Sparkford,
Nr Yeovil, Somerset BA22 7JJ, UK.

Tel: 01963 440635 Fax: 01963 440001
Int. tel: +44 1963 440635 Fax +44 1963 440001
E-mail: sales@haynes-manuals.co.uk
Web site: www.haynes.com.uk

Designed and typeset by G&M, Raunds, Northamptonshire
Printed and bound in Great Britain by J. H. Haynes and Co. Ltd, Sparkford

Contents

Acknowledgements

For the time that they set aside to discuss their thoughts, motivations and recollections in the preparation of this book I would like to offer grateful thanks to the following:

Gary Anderson; Rubens Barrichello; Nick Hayes; Doug Hayward, Bob and Jane Herbert; Johnny Herbert; Alan Jenkins; Allard Kalff; Ellen Kolby; Steve Madincea; Jan Magnussen; Andy Miller; Jac Nasser; Mark Perkins; Andrew Philpott; Neil Ressler; Joe Saward; Stuart and Di Spires; Jackie Stewart; Helen Stewart; Mark Stewart; Paul Stewart; John Valentine; Jos Verstappen; Martin Whitaker.

Introduction

The car that first turned me on to F1 was the BRM H16, a brutal mechanical blunder driven in the 1967 International Trophy race at Silverstone by Jackie Stewart. *Autocar's* race report carried a wonderful photo of the Scot charging head-on towards the photographer, the car's great orange-banded snout hunting hungrily through Copse corner.

As a driver Stewart experienced the entire gamut of emotions, from triumph to despair. In an international career that spanned a decade and yielded three World Championships, he and his wife Helen saw many of their close friends killed in action. Their lives were enriched by their success, but it came at a terrible price.

It seems inconceivable, looking back, that in 1968 *British* officials advised him that if he really wanted trees cut down in dangerous places at Brands Hatch, he could do it himself. The foundation of today's high level of safety throughout motorsport was laid by Stewart's tireless campaign of the Sixties and early Seventies. It was he who brought about the lining of circuits with Armco barrier; he who was in the vanguard of safety with seat belts, fireproof overalls, full-face helmets and sturdier rollover hoops; he who was never afraid to speak out when others were content to remain silent. He wore his crown with honour.

Yet many years later, when I met him for the first time, the memory bank is curiously blank. There is a reason for this. I well remember my first meeting with Mario Andretti not just because of the sheer charisma of the man, but because friends like to remind me it was one of the few occasions on which I have been stumped for something to say. I mean, what do you say on first acquaintance with a guy like that, that isn't going to sound dumb?

I know I met Jackie Stewart at Monaco sometime in the early Eighties, but his charisma took a different form, and he had precisely the opposite effect. Meeting him was no big deal, in one sense. He made you feel so at ease, included you even though you were on the fringe of the group of journalists with whom he was indulging in his customary banter. Within minutes he made you feel as if you'd been friends for years.

It's a rare gift, that. Every bit as rare as the gifts he exploited when he climbed into a race car, or when today he goes into a business meeting. It's a key part of an extraordinary character.

Stewart is an object lesson in how to graduate to F1 with style

Jackie Stewart is one of the few people I like to count as a friend in the F1 milieu, as opposed to one of those working acquaintances it's easy to mistake for a friend. For many years now a small group of us, JYS included, has taken to dining together in Montreal at Canadian GP time close to his birthday. Our first such get-together was a decade ago in a burger bar called Le Tramway, into which Stewart almost tiptoed, aghast. It was a no-frills kind of place, even the year that the language police were on patrol to ensure that the staff in such joints spoke French first and English preferably not at all. In time Jackie got his wish and subtly moved us upmarket, but the gathering remains what it always was. Not a glorified press conference, but just a dinner with a bunch of mates. I think he enjoys it as much as we do.

This honest informality is one of many endearing traits about a man who thrives on details. To watch him social-ising not just with F1 people but with their wives, during his charity shooting events at Gleneagles, is to watch a consummate pro at work. He has an uncanny ability to make everyone feel relaxed and the focus of attention.

At Silverstone one year he was introduced to two young boys. When he was jokingly told to get a move on by their father, as he paused in his autograph signing session to inquire how long they had been interested in motorsport and then shared with them the fact that he too had done what they were doing as a 10 year-old, he smiled tolerantly. 'If you get any more aggravation from your Father, give me a call,' he said, producing his business card for them. I know, I had to listen to them laughing about it all the way home. The Stewarts' sons, Paul and Mark, are the sort of likeable young men you'd be pleased to have your own boys grow up into. In character, they are unspoiled credits to their parents.

When Jackie and Paul set up Paul Stewart Racing they set new standards that others have been obliged to follow. The creation of Stewart Grand Prix has been an object lesson in how to graduate to F1 in the proper manner, doing things by the book yet with style. It is not the only team happy to open

Happiness is … in Malaysia the author celebrates a sartorial breakthrough and the GP of Europe victory with Jackie and Paul Stewart, Johnny Herbert and Rubens Barrichello. Not a kilt in sight … (LAT)

its accounts to any potential investor, but you might be surprised how few really would be that candid.

It's easy for cynics to regard the Stewarts as too squeaky clean to be true, Wallace and Grommit go F1 (wearing The Wrong – albeit impeccably tailored – Trousers). And there are some who have found dealing with them more than just a trial. When Jackie Stewart wants something you know about it, and he gets it. There have been several occasions when the air on the Stewart and Ford sides of the camp has been tense. But you speak as you find. To me, the qualities they have brought are a breath of fresh air for F1. The sale to Ford Motor Company, while a surprise as far as the actual timing was concerned, was the logical progression, the final step forward. Typically, by the standards of F1 in the Nineties, it was trend-setting.

In his career as a driver Jackie set a new record of 27 Grands Prix wins prior to retirement in 1973. It was therefore intensely gratifying that, with but three races left before the Stewart name was replaced by Jaguar for 2000, Johnny Herbert racked up victory number 28 in the Grand Prix of Europe at the Nurburgring. Those of us who regard integrity as an asset thoroughly enjoyed that historic day, perhaps the more so because it also put that loyal underdog Englishman back in the spotlight.

There was an amusing corollary. Jackie set himself up as something of an authority on sartorial elegance on his return to F1, and frequently made disparaging remarks about the colourful Tommy Hilfiger shirts that were one of the few material things I got out of my time working for Team Lotus in the early Nineties. Of course, it ill behoved a man who sported tartan pants to make such observations, but – no surprise – Jackie never quite saw it that way. At Monza in 1998 I bought a giant poster from Mario Acquati's shop at the height of this good-natured public banter. It revealed JYS back in 1973 in his full glory, nattily attired in a fawn corduroy suit complete with flared trousers. Unveiling this under the Stewart awning, I promised him I would wear my 'worst' Hilfiger shirt and a pair of tartan trews for a day when Stewart GP won its first race.

That day finally came in Malaysia. I had lost no time in communicating my measurements to Jackie on the Sunday evening of Nurburgring, but typically he was more thorough than to take my word for it. I was duly dispatched to his tailor, Doug Hayward, in Mayfair's Mount Street, to be measured properly. Och, Jackie even paid! Given what that first victory represented to all of the people at Stewart and Ford, and the way in which it brought a racing wheel full circle for the Stewart family and for myself, it was fun to join Wallace and Grommit and slip on Doug's beautifully cut wares after the Stewart-Fords had qualified fifth and sixth on Saturday. Unfortunately Jackie refused to accept that I was his illegitimate offspring come to claim his inheritance, but at least I hadn't offered to wear a kilt…

DAVID TREMAYNE
Harrow and Stapleton
November 1999

Chapter 1

A Scotsman on the make

If one were to seek the perfect ambassador for motorsport, John Young Stewart would be a leading candidate. Thrice champion of the world, tireless safety crusader, internationally known businessman, and founder of his own F1 team, his reputation spans the globe. Still as recognisably jaunty as he approached his 60th birthday as he was in his heyday as the world's best racing driver, the little Scot remained a fundamentally modest and kind man driven by the need to excel, yet smart enough to let his countless achievements speak for themselves. Others may fret about their place in their chosen society, but Stewart has always had the nous to let others draw the conclusions about him and place him into his proper perspective. Though he is, of course, adept at shaping the opinions of others!

In 99 Grands Prix starts, Jackie Stewart secured 27 victories and lost more through capricious circumstance. He won three Drivers' World Championships and took countless successes in racing categories outside F1, and his hallmark was the cleanliness, economy and precision of his work at the wheel. He had no need to push any other driver off the circuit to achieve his goal.

Stewart's brother Jimmy, eight years his senior, raced a D Type Jaguar in the '50s, and Jackie became a devotee. 'It was terrific to go around with him with the autograph book when I was 10. I was an enormous fan of racing, long before I did it myself. I got autographs from people such as Fangio and Ascari, Jean Behra, Harry Schell, Froilan Gonzales, Louis Rosier, Ken Wharton, Reg Parnell. It all meant a great deal to me at that age.' His own competitive urges, however, were initially satisfied by clay pigeon shooting, and by the age of 14 in 1953 he had won his first trophy in a straight competition with adults. His grandfather had been a gamekeeper, and his father was a crack shot, and for a young boy who found

The grandson of a gamekeeper, wee John Young Stewart shows off an early catch. (Phipps/Sutton)

school difficult shooting proved a blessed relief. 'It felt fantastic, because up to then I'd never done anything in my life that anybody had given me any praise for. That was the very beginning, and then I went on to shoot for Scotland.'

The family lived in Dumbuck, a village near Loch Lomond in Scotland, by the garage business that his father had built up. Jackie worked there from the age of 15 to 23, and today one of his oldest friends, John Lindsay, still lives in the house in which Stewart was born. From its roof as a child he would watch the big ships, the *Queen Elizabeth* and the *Queen Mary*, passing down the Clyde on their way from the shipyards.

At the garage his duties included preparing other people's cars for racing, among them a Marcos GT owned by Barry Filer. By the time he had finished, every part sparkled. His own career began modestly; after he had been invited to try a customer's Porsche in a sprint, Filer put him behind the wheel of the Marcos. Stewart had narrowly lost out on a place in the Olympic shooting squad, and the failure had crushed him; now he found something that could take shooting's place. 'I never had big ideas

Stewart wins the Coupe des Nations and proves himself a crack shot, but failure to make the Olympic team of 1960 would prove to have far-reaching consequences for both the shooting and motor racing worlds. (Phipps/Sutton)

A committed professional

At the height of Jackie Stewart's safety crusade, one journalist dubbed him a 'milk and water' driver, whatever that meant. Denis Jenkinson, of *Motor Sport*, vilified him for the stance he took, and for forcing circuit owners away from the view that it was just too bad if drivers left the track and struck trees. For Jenkinson, an ultimate purist, that was all part of the risk, the appeal of a visceral sport. And he had earned his right to such an entrenched viewpoint after riding as passenger to the World Champion motorcycle and sidecar racer Eric Oliver, and as navigator to Stirling Moss in their historic triumph on the 1955 Mille Miglia.

One day in 1966 had changed Stewart's entire outlook.

There were two circuits that he came to loathe from the safety point of view: Spa-Francorchamps and the Nurburgring. Both offered fantastic challenges to racing drivers, yet each was a minefield of traps awaiting the careless or the unlucky.

During the opening lap of the Belgian GP in June 1966 a sudden rain shower part way round the 8-mile circuit left the terrifyingly fast Masta Straight awash, yet the field had started on a dry road 3 miles earlier. In those days there were no radio links, and half the field spun off when drivers suddenly encountered the unexpectedly slippery surface. One of them was Stewart, who lay trapped and soaked in leaking fuel as his BRM ended up in a ditch. The incident made a huge impression on him, and thereafter he launched himself energetically into the campaign for racing safety, for which one could read common sense. Yet his driving never suffered, especially at Spa and Nurburgring. Ever the professional, he always shone at both.

In 1967 he drove one of his greatest races at Spa in the recalcitrant BRM H16. It was heavier than a hangover, but at least it could stretch its legs at Spa and Stewart had it going as never before. He was a potential winner until a gearshift problem arose and he had to give best to the American Dan Gurney in his Eagle Weslake. Driving the hefty monster with one hand, while holding it in gear at more than 160mph with the other, Stewart finished an honourable second. That day, it was almost as good as a win.

At the Nurburgring in 1968 he scored the greatest win of his career, streaking his Matra home an astonishing 4 minutes ahead of the field in a race run in rain and fog. To win at the 'Ring was truly the mark of greatness, yet he had no qualms about admitting his detestation for the place.

'I never did a lap of the Nurburgring that I didn't have to do. I defy anyone to say they really liked it, if they went properly quick there.'

Jackie Stewart never shrank from voicing his opinions, however unpopular they might have been. And even those who subscribed to the 'milk and water' condemnation were forced to concede that, whatever his personal views about a circuit, he never once drew back from giving his utmost commitment once he was in the cockpit.

of where it would lead,' he says. 'It just seemed a terrific thing to do.'

He did it well. Before long he was racing for the famous Ecurie Ecosse. He'd hit the Big Time, with *the* Scottish team. The team that had won Le Mans with its D Types in the '50s.

After rising star Timmy Mayer had been killed early in 1964, respected entrant Ken Tyrrell began looking for another driver. Stewart was a potential candidate.

'Bruce McLaren set Ken's F3 Cooper up at Goodwood and recorded a lap time. I'd never driven a single-seater before but I was quicker when I had my turn. I'd called Jimmy Clark to ask him should I do it, because I never thought I would become a serious driver. I thought my life was going to be in my father's garage. But Jimmy said that if I wanted to be a racing driver I had to drive single-seaters. When Bruce improved, so did I. Ken told me I didn't need to go quick, but I was just driving the way I usually did, without risking going off the road.'

Stewart didn't see it as anything other than a big thrill. Certainly, he never expected it to lead anywhere. But he and Tyrrell quickly agreed terms, and the decision paid off almost immediately when Stewart won the prestigious F3 race that supported the Monaco Grand Prix. It was by far his most important success to date, the one that really set him on the road.

'The funny thing is that I didn't have enough money to get down to Monaco. I stayed with Bruce McLaren the night before; everyone else flew down to Monte Carlo but I didn't have

Me and my brother. In 1964 the emergent Jackie poses with his Ecurie Ecosse Tojeiro coupé, alongside elder brother Jimmy and his Jaguar D Type. (Phipps/Sutton)

enough for that so I had to drive down with Helen. I remember I left my briefcase on the roof of the car when I left his house. I got to Dover and found I had nothing! We had enough money for one return ticket, so Helen and I got two singles just to get us there. There was no money for a rental car, so we took the bus from Nice. I actually walked in to the circuit for two mornings and got a ride the third...'

His star was now in orbit. Though it seems incredible now, rather like Frank Williams letting Juan Pablo Montoya out for the first time in an F1 car during free practice for the British GP, Stewart's first taste of F1 came in precisely that manner. He drove Jimmy Clark's Lotus 33 for a few laps at Brands Hatch later that season, during Saturday practice for the British GP. 'Out of the blue Colin Chapman said why didn't I drive the car. I'm sure Jimmy had a lot to do with it. The gearchange pattern was the opposite way round, and I engaged second instead of fourth gear at Druids Bend and spun it, but I kept going. It was a big thrill.'

By now a lot of teams were clamouring for his signature on a contract for 1965, among them BRM, Cooper and Lotus. The equivalent today would be McLaren, Williams and Jordan all fighting over an F3 graduate such as Jenson Button.

Later still that heady season, Clark slipped a disc during a snowball fight when Ford launched its Cortina down a bobsleigh run, and suddenly

Side by side at Monza in 1965, Stewart and his BRM team-mate Graham Hill fight for victory. Jackie won when Graham made an error, to score the first of 27 GP successes. (Phipps/Sutton)

At Monaco a year later Stewart took his second victory, and the first of three in the Principality. His next win would be a long time coming, however… (Phipps/Sutton)

His Matra-Ford still equipped with the upright-mounted aerofoils that would soon be banned, Stewart opened his title-winning 1969 season in style with an easy victory at Kyalami. (Phipps/Sutton)

Little did either father or son Paul know what lay on the road ahead, here at Monza in 1969, when Jackie clinched his first World Championship with a narrow victory. (Phipps/Sutton)

Chapman was calling upon Stewart to make his F1 debut for Lotus in the Rand Grand Prix at Kyalami. By then he had already signed for BRM for 1965, but team manager Tony Rudd wisely reasoned that he might as well let his new charge make his preliminary mistakes in somebody else's car, especially as BRM hadn't entered. Stewart took pole position for his first F1 race, but a driveshaft sheared at the start of the first heat. He won the second convincingly after setting fastest lap while battling with team-mate Mike Spence and former champion Graham Hill. In the space of a season he had gone from sportscars with Ecurie Ecosse to F3, then up to F1, almost without drawing breath.

He had decided to join BRM because he wasn't ultimately confident that Colin Chapman wouldn't favour Clark, with whom he had already won one championship title. Chapman offered Jackie a deal, then doubled it once and once again when Stewart continued to resist. Jackie took the view that if the original could so easily have been multiplied, it was wiser to go elsewhere.

He and Clark shared an apartment in London, which they called the Scottish Embassy. They were extremely good friends, but one incident brought home to Stewart just how much progress he was making. 'I drove a Lotus Elan against Jimmy at Silverstone. I didn't know where to brake at Stowe, but he wouldn't tell me. This was the first time I thought, "Hello. If Jimmy doesn't want to tell me where to brake he must be worried…"' It was, in its way, a significant compliment, an indication that he was a man to be reckoned with. Over the course of the following season the only driver who could hold a candle to Clark as he romped to his second World Championship was his fellow countryman.

'In a car Jim Clark was everything I aspired to be,' Stewart says today. 'He was a very nice man, very gentle, very well-mannered. Introverted; not extroverted at all. He was unusual in many respects in that way. He was unsure of himself, indecisive outside of a racing car. He used to ruin evenings in restaurants, movies, anything, because he couldn't decide what to do. But he was a lovely man. A lovely man.'

Stewart's first Grand Prix for BRM came at East London in 1965, where he scored a point on his debut by finishing sixth in the South African GP. He was well pleased, though Tyrrell was out of pocket having bet Bruce McLaren that Jackie would finish ahead of him. Bruce was fifth, Jackie a place behind after a poor start…

The first victory was not long coming, as Stewart headed for the non-championship International Trophy race at Silverstone in May. He had bolstered his South African result with second place in the Race of Champions at Brands Hatch in March and pole position for Goodwood's *Sunday Mirror* Trophy in April. Now he took on and beat reigning World Champion John Surtees and Ferrari. When Hill and Jack Brabham dropped out, the young pretender found himself pressured by the old campaigner. Surtees slipped ahead once, before Stewart fought back to win by 3 seconds. He was on his way.

There were no team orders but I worried I'd done the wrong thing

---

He led the Monaco GP for five laps before finishing third, and was then second to Clark at Spa, Clermont-Ferrand and Zandvoort. In between there was fifth at Brands Hatch, and the first accident, an off during the German GP at Nurburgring. Then came Monza, and his first GP win. Today, his bitter-sweet memories are confirmation of his integrity.

'It was terrific, a fantastic feeling to win. But it was a mixed feeling too, because I was frightened that I had done something wrong with Graham. I hadn't, but we were left fighting for the victory and I beat him. He made a mistake and went on the marbles, and I went inside. There were no team orders, but I was slightly perturbed that I might have done the wrong thing. He was very good, though, and told me I had won fair and square.'

And so the story went on. A year later he won in Monaco, and nearly added the Indianapolis 500 until his Lola broke its engine close to the end. There was a small consolation later in the year when he took the same car to victory in the Fuji 200 USAC race. After a disastrous 1967 season with BRM's uncompetitive H16 he joined Tyrrell's nascent Matra-Ford F1 effort for 1968, narrowly missing a championship that later he said he had not been ready for. Had he not missed races after breaking his scaphoid in an F2 accident, the story could have been very different. In 1969 everything came together, and Tyrrell's new Matra-Ford crushed its opposition. After a false start with March in 1970, after Matra had withdrawn, they bounced back with the eponymous Tyrrell in 1971 before Stewart developed an ulcer that laid him low for key races in 1972. That year he finished runner-up to Emerson Fittipaldi, who had inherited the mantle of the

1970 would be a lean year as Tyrrell was forced to switch from Matra to March, yet Stewart managed victory in the Spanish GP at Jarama. (Phipps/Sutton)

departed Clark and Rindt at Lotus.

The 1973 season would be Stewart's last as a racing driver. He knew the odds against survival, and, since 1970, 1972 had been the only season in which an F1 driver had not perished in an accident. The sport had repaid him well in terms of material reward, but also exacted a high price.

'Helen and I once counted the friends we had lost in racing,' he admits, 'and stopped when we got beyond 50. It was just a terrible time, with so many people losing their lives. It just didn't make sense to me.'

His sons Paul and Mark were still small, Paul a rising eight, Mark five.

Once, Paul had come back from school in Switzerland and shaken his mother rigid when, with all the innocence of youth, he had asked Helen Stewart when his Daddy was going to die. Jochen Rindt and Jo Bonnier had died, and Natasha Rindt and Joakim and Jonas Bonnier went to the same school. Somebody had mentioned to Paul that if you were a racing driver, you got killed.

'When I think back,' Jackie admits, 'it's remarkable how well Helen coped. I think she did a great job and handled it in a really mature way. She managed to isolate herself. I think back to the number of hotel rooms she had to go

into, to pack the things for a wife whose husband had been killed. Drivers today just don't understand that side of the sport.'

Stewart invested more than he received in return. Without his unflinching safety crusade in the 1960s, the sport would never have progressed from the senseless risk-taking of the days before Armco barriers protected drivers from trees. There is no question that many drivers survived who would not otherwise have escaped from accidents on circuits where Stewart's plea for tree-paring or barrier-erection had dramatically increased the margin for error. 'I'm proud to have been part of that progress,' he says today.

In defeat he was gracious, and even though Clay Regazzoni's tactics in Germany in 1972 left him outraged he retained his outward composure. In victory he wasn't the type to crow. Looking back, he has been there, he has seen it, and he has won the victory cup. But he was there in the darkest times, he saw it from the depths, it was he who peered into the blackest pit that can sometimes be motor racing. Throughout he did so with style and courage worthy of a champion. Perhaps even more remarkably, he did it all without recourse to the tricks of malice, controversy or dishonesty.

At the end of 1973, the year in which Jackie won his third and last

Well into his stride once the bugs had been ironed out of Ken Tyrrell's eponymous car, Stewart crushed Ferrari during the 1971 French GP as he headed for his second title. (Phipps/Sutton)

23

In victory (here at Zandvoort in 1969), in defeat or in sorrow, Helen Stewart was never far from her husband's side. (Phipps/Sutton)

title, his team-mate François Cevert was killed during practice at Watkins Glen in America for what should have been Stewart's 100th and last GP. The Frenchman's death was violent and horrible, but it came far too late to influence Stewart's decision to retire.

'I had made that in April that year. Helen never knew. I only told Ken Tyrrell, and Walter Hayes and John Waddell at Ford. We had lunch in London but I didn't want anyone else to know. I didn't want Helen thinking of ten green bottles... I didn't tell her until the afternoon that François died. Even François didn't know. He was thinking of leaving Ken; an offer from Ferrari was tickling him. Without letting him know I was going, I told him he needed one more year with me... I

think he would have won the championship in 1974 for Ken.'

Jackie Stewart's achievements were not limited to the race track. Many young lads in the East End were grateful for his work with the Springfield Boys' Club, while his fund-raising on behalf of racing mechanics, via the Grand Prix Mechanics' Charitable Trust, benefited many who would otherwise have suffered financial hardship. Such efforts always echo that old adage that no sight is more impressive than a Scotsman on the make! His work with Ford, Goodyear and latterly Bridgestone has led to generations of safer road cars.

He achieved all this despite being told at school that he was a dunce because he found the work so onerous.

It was not until he had retired from driving that he came to realise that he was dyslexic. Son Paul is, too. Like every other problem he has tackled in life, Stewart has faced his own dyslexia with determined resilience.

In the '60s he embraced fashions wholeheartedly, and the Beatles cap, long hair and dark sunglasses became his trademarks. Today, the natty Racing Stewart tartan trews and cap again leave no doubt of his identity.

Back then sportsmen were more polite and likely to offer meaningful comment to the media ('meeja' in Stewart-speak). But even in today's 'sound bite' era of 10-second attention spans and brusque, sportsman's arro-gance, he remains a gentleman who understands how to conduct himself properly. Unusually, he retains a strong sense of, and reverence for, history, the thread that ultimately unites all drivers when their racing careers are finished.

His acumen and integrity have become the stuff of legend. The relationship between Stewart and entrant Ken Tyrrell was one of the greatest in the sport's history, yielding 25 GP victories and those three titles. 'Ken's decision-making was always immediate and positive. He'd say, "Let's do this." And do it. Everything was imminent, there wasn't any soft time,' Stewart recalls.

Yet only a handshake was ever needed to seal their deals.

The relationship between Stewart and François Cevert was like younger and older brother. On more than one occasion in 1973 Jackie felt that the dashing Frenchman could have beaten him, and with the entire Tyrrell team he was devastated when Cevert died during practice for what should have been his own final Grand Prix.
(Phipps/Sutton)

By the time he took his third victory at Monaco in 1973 Stewart had already made the decision to retire at the end of the season, but fewer than a handful of people knew at this stage. (Phipps/Sutton)

'After my first test with Ken he took me home. That night he offered me a contract. He'd pay me £10,000, but he wanted 10 per cent of my earnings over the next five or ten years. I wasn't sure, so he said the alternative was that I'd still have the drive, but he'd pay me £5 to make the contract legal.

'I was very excited all night, having driven faster than Bruce, who was a hero. The next day I told Ken I wasn't sure about the long-term contract, but I'd take the £5! And I had no money! I turned down £10,000! But it was the

right decision for me, and it paid off.'

When he decided to do F1 with Tyrrell for 1968, he was being courted heavily by Ferrari, and had shaken hands with Enzo Ferrari himself, the Old Man. 'But I had trust in Ken. I thought it just seemed the right thing to do. Everything else was just so complicated, and the Ford engine was so simple, so small. It just seemed the right thing to do. The Matra chassis was extraordinary. I knew Ken could do the administration, I knew he could do the infrastructure and had the right people. I knew it was the right decision. The only dilemma was Ferrari: I don't care who you are, to a racing car driver Ferrari is Ferrari... But the experience I had with them so underlined the purity of the Tyrrell relationship. I nearly went to Ferrari. I was very close to going there as team-mate to

Arise, Sir Jackie?

Over the years newspaper readers have become used to knighthoods bestowed apparently willy-nilly in the world of the performing arts. Men whose ability to pretend to be someone else appears never to have ceased to attract those in a position to bestow such honours.

Even in the equestrian world, which is admittedly the Queen and the Queen Mother's chosen sport, the revelation that a *commentator* of the noble art of horse racing was to be dubbed by Her Majesty scarcely raised an eyebrow. Not a competitor, you understand, or a breeder – a commentator.

Motorsport has generated the engineering ability that has made Britain the envy of nations, but has enjoyed slim pickings. Until Frank Williams's achievements were finally recognised late in 1998, Sir Jack Brabham had been the last man knighted for his services to motor racing. Speedkings such as George Eyston, John Cobb, Donald Campbell, Richard Noble and Andy Green were signally overlooked, even though the inter-war days of British glory in land speed record breaking saw Major Henry Segrave and Captain Malcolm Campbell's achievements acknowledged with knighthoods.

When his remarkable career, his unpublicised charitable work and his ongoing contribution to the sport – both on the track and in the realm of safety – are taken into account, It must surely be only a matter of time before John Young Stewart is invited to join such elite company.

A close friend of Princess Anne, Stewart has provided employment for her unassuming son Peter Phillips on several occasions since Stewart GP began racing. (Sutton)

The changing face of success: the 1967-model Stewart retains short back and sides (above left), but two years later the distinctive long-haired style had taken over. (Phipps/Sutton)

Sometimes it does not always pay to be reminded of the fashions of yore… (Phipps/Sutton)

Stewart was not remotely tempted by a lucrative offer to return full-time to the cockpit in 1979, but did a series of F1 car tests for Autocar *in the late '80s. Here he tries the Benetton B187 turbocar at Oulton Park.* (Phipps/Sutton)

Chris Amon. And it would have been a mistake. I didn't have the authority. I think you've got to go to Ferrari as an authority, not as a promising guy. Even then I realised that. Being with a strong team-mate never worried me, even Jimmy Clark. I would have gone with Jimmy to Lotus because I think I would have learned something from him, but the reason I didn't do that was because I needed Colin and I knew only one person who had Colin's focus. Jimmy. And at Ferrari I thought I would always be having to look over my shoulder.'

This, then, was the man who said that retiring in 1973 was the best decision he ever made in a full life. There

was an offer to come back to F1 in 1979, which was serious, but not serious enough to tempt him to give it consideration. There was no point. He was already deriving as much satisfaction from his business life as he had drawn from racing.

When the lure of F1 finally did prove too strong, it was for entirely different reasons. Events in his life had shaped his destiny in a way he could never have envisaged in 1973, or in 1979. Events that would place son Paul

on the racetrack, and that would again lead the family name into Victory Lane.

In 1996 Jackie Stewart would finally bring his clear-headed thinking to bear on setting up his own F1 team, after years of speculation. And as Stewart Grand Prix headed for the track in 1997 it would do so with a style and professionalism that set a fresh example to those who aspired to follow, and indeed to some who were already there.

Chapter 2

A different way
of doing things

Robin Congdon was a presentable young man, presumably American since his reference forms said that his education had been completed at Duke University in North Carolina. During tests at the Brands Hatch Racing School his lap times weren't bad. Indeed, instructors there told Stirling Moss, who was visiting, that the guy seemed pretty good. If Stirling had actually bumped into Robin that day in 1986, he would have understood why, because he would have recognised him.

Robin Congdon was very pleased that they hadn't come across one another, for Robin Congdon was really Paul Stewart, Jackie's 21-year-old son.

'I used the name of Robin Congdon, a friend at University, because though I'd caught the racing bug I'd never actually done it properly, and there was no reason to assume I could do it,' Paul explained. 'My father and I felt it was the right thing to go to the Brands Hatch school under an assumed name.

If I'd gone there as Son of Jackie, they might have treated me differently and I wanted to be treated absolutely like everyone else. When I saw Stirling arrive during my last day there I immediately turned away so he wouldn't recognise me. I wasn't sure if he'd seen me so I called him later to explain, just in case. I was quite chuffed that they said I'd been good…'

Jackie and Helen Stewart were not so chuffed at the idea of their elder son taking up motorsport. When he was 17 Paul had voiced the idea and Jackie had gently dissuaded him, offering to help later providing that he completed his university education first.

'In any case he'd done so much for me that I didn't want to go against him,' Paul admitted. 'I knew that the idea of putting his son through university was very important to him. And I think he felt he'd got away with it, until I came back from my Political Science studies at Duke and told him I still wanted to do a racing school.'

32

Typically, they discussed the subject at great length, and agreed that Brands Hatch was the ideal starting point. Like most parents, Jackie and Helen hoped that having a go might dispel some of the glamour around the idea and get it out of his system. Instead, Paul got the bug badly. By 1987, the year in which a young blond kid from Romford by the name of Johnny Herbert was preparing to ravage the British F3 Championship in a Reynard run by Eddie Jordan, he was looking at a season of Formula Ford. He launched his campaign in London, and in a telling piece of unselfish common sense Jackie deliberately stayed away. It was to be Paul's project and Paul's day. The Stewart name had undoubtedly helped Paul to find his sponsor, and equally it was the hook that brought many of the national newspaper journalists along when otherwise the majority would have had no interest whatsoever, but Jackie was determined that his own presence was not going to overshadow the proceedings. It was not an easy decision.

Few who gathered to hear the news actually knew Paul, certainly not as the young adult who stood on the stage before them. Some had memories of the small kid who was with his father during Jackie's racing days, others didn't know him from Adam. But he made a big impression.

Clear-voiced and confident, Paul began his address. When the occasional titters became guffaws and tipped him off to something happening

A family affair: Paul has maximum emotional back-up at Snetterton in 1987, as he makes his motor racing debut in Formula Ford 1600. (Sutton)

behind him, he dealt with a potentially embarrassing situation with aplomb that was quite remarkable.

His sponsor was a company called The Carphone Group. Large white polystyrene letters on a blue board in the background proclaimed this as Paul spoke, but it was a warm room and every so often one letter would lose its fight to remain glued in place. Before long Paul's sponsor had been reduced to T-e C-rp-n- Gr-up. It was the nightmare scenario: a young fellow trying to make an impression, and an embarrassing development that threatened to turn the whole thing into farce. It was

fast approaching one of those child talent shows where the kid starts singing, forgets the words, and flees with hands covering face.

But not Paul Stewart.

Eventually, against his natural inclination, he turned to see what was causing the merriment, and discovered the awful truth. And that was when everyone in the room realised that, despite his tender years, Paul Stewart was no pushover. Turning back to his audience, who now felt entitled to laugh openly without any polite attempt to disguise their amusement at the situation, he said calmly: 'As you know, my

He acquitted himself well in the Van Diemen, even if he did hate the mandatory series-sponsor stickers... (Sutton)

father and I are both dyslexic. Now you know what I see when I read the words The Carphone Group.'

It was a brilliant off-the-cuff remark and it didn't just kill the laughter, it broke the ice and earned an appreciative and hearty round of applause. After that the launch was a roaring success and he got column inches by the score.

'To be honest, when I look back I'm just amused by the apparent seriousness of it all,' Paul admitted years later. 'But we got fantastic coverage from the launch and my initial races; it taught me all about the value of publicity.'

In his first season he did well. His Van Diemen was smartly turned out in the dark blue of Scotland, and he

started as he meant to go on. 'It was always important to me to do things properly. I used to make my mechanic wear smart trousers, which he hated! I was always very proud of the presentation and I hated having to use the mandatory Townsend Thoresen championship stickers on the car; they looked such a mess. Professionalism was always the key, and it's always important to get the details right. Once you develop your method of doing things, that's what you carry through with you and it's important to give that consistent message all the time. If you start scruffy, that's how you remain.'

He took his first victory, and by 1988, the year in which the Camel cigarette brand managers opted for an orgy of nepotism by signing sons of famous racing fathers, he was ready for the next step up, Formula Ford 2000. Now his Reynard chassis was painted in Camel yellow, as was the support van and trailer. Professionalism again. But now there was something else, too. The evolution of the team that would lead the Stewarts back to F1: Paul Stewart Racing.

Paul and Jackie didn't feel that there was an existing team that could service Paul's needs properly. They were wealthy, and there were plenty of teams out there all too happy to indulge in a bit of subtle redistribution of that wealth. There was just too much potential to be taken advantage of, and that was complete anathema to the triple World Champion. That left one option: to set up their own team. And who better to become the first employee than Roy Topp, who had

A year later Helen was among the team members who greeted his arrival at Heathrow for the launch of Paul Stewart Racing and its venture into Formula Ford 2000. (Sutton)

formerly been Jackie's mechanic? Paul well remembers the day when he was first brought together with his own racing team.

'I'd been in the States and flew in to Heathrow, where this smart outfit of truck and trailer was waiting for me. I arrived and there it was! I have a favourite photograph of the equipment, and a family shot with my brother Mark and my mother.' Again, Jackie had absented himself.

He was cautious about the reasons for forming Paul Stewart Racing as a full-blown race team rather than the structure behind which Paul had operated in 1987. In retrospect it's easy to see this as the first deliberate step towards F1, but Jackie was always at pains to try and dissuade observers from such a point of view at the time.

'I certainly never assumed that,' he says. 'Yes, it was logical in some respects. But when I looked at one particular Formula 1 opportunity, I wasn't ready for it. I wouldn't have been capable of running it. I had an awful lot to learn about racing teams. I went on to learn an enormous amount from FF2000 and F3, an awful lot from Opel Lotus and F3000. I don't think many people had got that many in one package. It was a fantastically fast learning curve; we knew we would make mistakes and then make some more, but I would be able to learn more positively from my mistakes than if I had naively jumped into a Formula 1 operation where mistakes are a lot more expensive. I wasn't ready for it back then, and I'm not shy to admit it.'

Detractors sneered at the apparent

ease with which Paul Stewart had been able to make the graduation from aspirant to race driver, for motorsport can be every bit as bitchy off the track as it is competitive on it. Sponsorship is always hard to find. But Paul earned his slice of Camel's budget, and his income from other sponsors, the hard way. He would drive the team van up and down the motorways, moving from one Ford dealership to another at the opposite end of the country, then load everything up again and head off for a test session somewhere in between before driving back to base.

'There was a lot of driving, and it was a busy time, and all the while I was asking myself whether I was doing the right thing running a team and trying to be a driver. But my father liked the idea of building a company because up until then he'd always been a one-man band. I liked the idea too. We were happy to work together, because our relationship has always been close. There was a mutual desire to create something, though neither of us had dreams then of it becoming an F1 team.'

In particular, both of them would come to feel over and again how important it had been to go through that growing cycle as Paul Stewart Racing began to forge its reputation. They were learning, and they were prepared to start at the bottom and work their way up a step at a time.

As a driver, Paul showed winning speed and flair, and was ready for another move upwards in 1989, when Camel was among the sponsors who helped him into an F3 Reynard. It was a tough year, with drivers of the calibre of Mika Hakkinen (who would win the F1 World Championship in 1998), Allan McNish (who would later win

A new team meant a new logo. (Sutton)

Le Mans), Sir Jack Brabham's son David, the talented Swede Rickard Rydell, whose main successes would come later in Touring Cars, and British hopefuls such as Derek Higgins and the fast but always underfunded Gary Ward. Against these guys Paul was woefully inexperienced, and the media were not always kind. He would come to appreciate that publicity is a two-edged sword. But as the year progressed he regularly eclipsed his team-mate Otto Rensing, a young German whom PSR had taken on in the expectation that he would spearhead the team's results.

Their philosophy was simple – good preparation is key to success

---

Today, PSR's name is synonymous with F3 success, but Paul would open its account in unusual style at Snetterton that year. Few people have won races by crossing the finish line backwards…

'Dyslexia rules, KO!' Paul laughs today. 'I had a lot of stick from my friends for that, but at least it's a race people remember.'

As a sign of his growing maturity he'd been second fastest in qualifying, but because there had been sessions for two separate groups and some felt that it was unsafe because he had never started from the front row before, the times were split and the grid was formed by taking alternate times. This put Hakkinen and Brabham on the front row and left a slightly disgruntled Stewart only third, with McNish for company. Hakkinen made a blatant jump start, and both Brabham and McNish stalled, so though he was running second on the road to Hakkinen, Stewart knew he was leading the race because the Finn would be penalised.

'Derek Higgins was behind me,' Paul recalls, 'but I was driving well and had things under control. Russell corner was flat then if the car was right, but it wasn't easy. It was a great feeling to get it right. I knew on the first lap that if I was going to win I had to do Russell flat, so I just kept my foot down and did it. After that every subsequent lap there was just straightforward.'

Hakkinen, meanwhile, had spun and thrown dirt over the track while overturning his car. As Paul approached Russell towards the end of the race, he had a backmarker just ahead of him. 'I knew if I backed off that Higgins would have the momentum to pass me by the first corner, so I remained committed. The backmarker's car twitched one way and I moved to pass him on the other side. But he had twitched because, unseen by me, he was signalling that he was going to pull over the same way to let me by. I had to make a split second decision, reacted, and then I went on to the grass avoiding him and spun. Because of Hakkinen's accident, however, they were planning to stop the race even as I spun and crossed the line backwards.'

The result was backdated a lap because of the stoppage, so Paul Stewart Racing's first F3 victory was secure. Since that day in 1989 the team

The Staircase
of Talent

The principle was quite simple: Jackie and Paul Stewart aspired to create a means whereby drivers could progress through the ranks with PSR, from the GM Lotus Euroseries, through F3 and up to F3000. Jackie called it 'The Staircase of Talent'.

'In some cases we spot drivers at a very early age, maybe only 12 or 14. Others may join us when they are 17 or 18,' he outlined. 'Others still may be quite experienced by the time they arrive. There's certainly no shortage of applicants.'

'The idea is unique,' Paul said. 'A staircase that allows individuals to learn and then to move on and up the staircase.'

Some of the more successful graduates include Gil de Ferran, David Coulthard, Jan Magnussen and Dario Franchitti. Others, notably Canadian F3000 racer John Jones and Italian Marco Apicella, found the steps too steep. The latter made the fatal mistake of giving up during an F3000 race at Spa one year, which earned him a feisty rebuke from Jackie. 'He said the car was undriveable when he pulled into the pits,' Stewart said with incredulity. 'I told him, "Jesus Christ, you think this is undriveable? I had to drive the L&M Lola in the CanAm!"'

The Brazilian Gil de Ferran (below, with Paul and Jackie) was F3 champion for PSR in 1992, while David Coulthard (bottom) graduated through the PSR ranks from Vauxhall Lotus to F3000, via F3. (Sutton)

has gone on to win many F3 races, including the prestigious non-championship Macau GP – the jewel in the F3 crown – and the championship on six occasions. In doing so it has boosted the careers of Gil de Ferran, Kelvin Burt, Jan Magnussen, Dario Franchitti, David Coulthard, Ralph Firman, Johnny Kane, Mario Haberfield, Luciano Burti and Peter Dumbreck, to name but a few. From the modest start with a single-car team, PSR has grown to occupy 16,000sq ft of factory space on an estate in Milton Keynes, and to employ more than 45 people.

In 1992 PSR moved simultaneously into F3000, the rung of the racing ladder just below F1, with Paul and fellow Scot David Coulthard. Again,

success there was crucial in laying the foundation for Stewart Grand Prix, as PSR invested not just in Paul's future, but also, as Jackie described it, 'in the future of motor racing'.

'We now have one of the best-prepared racing teams in the world,' he continued, 'being served by some of the best technology available in motor racing. We have a tremendously broad range of visitors coming to see what we're doing differently, in our work-shops, at our races and at our functions.'

All down the line they had a simple philosophy: good preparation is the key to continued success. 'It's the single most important ingredient. It helps set the car up, and it adds to the security

In 1989 W. Duncan Lee (left) outlined Camel's plans to back Paul and Otto Rensing (right) as Paul Stewart Racing took the step up again, this time to Formula 3. (Sutton)

Paul's Reynard 893 is pointing the right way here before the start at Silverstone, but when his first F3 victory came at Snetterton in 1989 the yellow and blue car would cross the line backwards. (Sutton)

and confidence of the driver. We'll tell our mechanics, "Get your preparation absolutely right – if you do that we have a much better chance of winning." We tell our drivers, "Get your preparation done, well in advance of the corner, then you can be wonderfully creative in the corner. But if you arrive at the corner without good preparation every corner will be an adventure. And when you're having adventures in racing cars, it can only lead to one thing – you eventually end up off the track."'

Jackie stressed how PSR's mechanics grew with the company, the way that the drivers did. 'Often the mechanics' relationships with drivers last many years. My chief mechanic at Tyrrell, who won all three World

In the thick of it, Paul nonetheless had a difficult F3 season in 1990. (Sutton)

Championships for me, was Roger Hill. Roger was an extraordinary man. I don't think he ever perceived what value he added. He was better at what he did than I ever was at what I did. Good mechanics are geniuses.'

PSR's prospectus in the mid-1990s was a predictably glamorous production, which outlined its racing programme and ended with a key question: Will it take us into Formula 1?

'One day it may,' Paul suggested, and went on to say, 'If it does, it will be with a well-defined, sound business plan. Sound business reasons that will not

only help us continue to win races on the international circuits, but will also pay back our business partners handsomely.'

Jackie had always been very careful to play down any aspirations to go back into F1. So much so that in 1990, when he actively considered buying two teams, he was still playing his cards very close to his chest.

'We would never consider going F1 unless all of the circumstances were absolutely correct,' he reiterated, and chief among those was the engine supply situation. Stewart would surely

have considered other options, had they been available, but his prime target was naturally Ford, the company with which he had enjoyed such a long and healthy relationship. All along, both he and Paul knew that Ford was their best bet, and that if necessary they would simply have to bide their time.

Meanwhile, they looked at Lotus and Tyrrell. Both famous teams were ailing financially, which meant that their on-track results were also suffering. In the end, Peter Collins and Peter Wright took control at Lotus, to give it a four-year lease of life before the economic pitfalls of the sport finally

trapped them, while no deal could at that point be forged with Tyrrell. They would wait.

By 1993 they were ready to start planning properly for F1, and opened talks with John Barnard, one of the great designers of his time. Jackie reasoned that the Pacific Rim was becoming an ever more important market in world economics, and began his search for funding there. Right from the start, Malaysia played a key role in the planning. In a series of meetings with the Prime Minister, Dr Mahathir Mohamad, he devised a simple proposal: he and Paul would create a Malaysian F1 team and run it

Racing Stewart: the Tartan Army

Tartan has always featured in the Stewart story, since Jackie's helmet was adorned with a band of Royal Stewart, used by his ancestors preparing for battle. When Paul began racing he adopted Hunting Stewart, a darker tartan used in the manner its name suggests. A blend of the two was specially created for Stewart GP, another genuine tartan called Racing Stewart and officially recognised by The Scottish Tartan Society.

Pride in their Scottish background has always been a part of the Stewarts' racing careers. Jackie in particular makes big play of the 'Racing Stewart' tartan. At races he and Paul cut distinctive figures, wearing rather fetching trews of said hue as the final part of their image engineering.

out of the UK, using it to promote Malaysia's nascent car industry. They were seeking £24 million to get the ball rolling.

The Malaysians were certainly interested; Stewart's initial meeting was scheduled for 20 minutes but Dr Mohamad allowed it to run closer to an hour. Things gathered pace quickly, for the Malaysians were keen to enter F1 as early as 1996. They sent deputations to the UK to gather further information, and by happy coincidence they were at Thruxton when Paul Stewart Racing dominated the F3 race. But just as everything seemed to be going swimmingly it all fell apart; £24 million was just too much for the Government to stand at that time. 'It was tremendously disappointing, of course,' Jackie said. 'But there was no way we were going to succumb to the temptation to try and do it for less. That would have been fatal. If we couldn't do it properly, then we weren't going to do it at all.'

So the F1 idea went into mothballs again. Paul retired from racing that season, and focused his attention on looking closely at both IndyCars (as America's ChampCar series was then called) and the British Touring Car Championship. In the latter, he created a proposal to run Ford's work's effort. But though they were worthy categories, they just weren't F1.

Meanwhile, Ford helped Benetton to the World Championship in 1994, courtesy of Michael Schumacher and the small V8 Zetec-R power unit. But it was such a tragic – and ultimately controversial year – with the death of Ayrton Senna and Benetton being accused of cheating and using proscribed traction control, that Ford's greatest success since 1981 went almost unheralded. What summed it up was the advertisement that appeared the very week that the traction control row first began to surface. It ran a photograph of Ford's new EEC IV electronic control unit under the headline 'Who knows the secret of Ford's black magic box?' It was withdrawn almost immediately amid the furore.

There was another irony hidden

It helps to have friends. Duran Duran's Simon Le Bon and model wife Yasmin wish Paul well on the grid at Brands Hatch, 1991. (Sutton)

within this potential embarrassment. Nothing was ever found to suggest that Benetton had been breaking the rules, but in any case the team had bolder aspirations after colourful chief Flavio Briatore had been told late in 1993 that Ford would be looking elsewhere for a technical partner in 1995. No reasons were ever publicly divulged, but Ford was said to feel uncomfortable about Briatore's profile. Instead, as Benetton switched to the same Renault V10 engine as Williams, and used it to win a back-to-back championship, Ford turned to the quiet Swiss manufacturer, Peter Sauber. Jackie and Paul watched these developments with interest.

Jackie was good with a shotgun and gave Ford both barrels

Sauber was running the German driver Heinz-Harald Frentzen, who at that point in his career, before the downturn at Williams in 1997 and '98, was very highly rated. Indeed, his tag at that time was that of the 'man who was quicker than Schumacher', following their relative performances in the lower formulae. Sauber had come into F1 via sportscar racing, where it had been highly successful with Mercedes-Benz-powered cars that won the World Championship. For his first three seasons of F1 Peter Sauber continued to enjoy the support of Mercedes-Benz, but for 1995 the German giant switched to McLaren. The tie-up between Sauber and Ford appeared to be a marriage made in logic heaven, especially with Frentzen aboard. But the new V10 engine that Ford introduced for 1995 proved woefully uncompetitive. Even a season later, when Johnny Herbert was brought in to partner Frentzen in an effort to shore up Sauber's foundations by running two number one drivers, things failed to gel. Both drivers complained regularly about a lack of power, and Ford's embarrassment was compounded by the race-winning performance of Ferrari's first-ever V10 that was introduced at the beginning of the year.

The catalyst that the Stewarts had been awaiting finally appeared on 11 June 1995, fittingly enough Jackie's 56th birthday. He was in Canada doing his usual television work on the Grand Prix for CBC TV, and flew back to Detroit with Ford on other business. With him on the company's corporate jet was Neil Ressler, at that time Vice President of Advanced Vehicle Technology. He was deeply unhappy with Ford's F1 involvement and during the flight sought Stewart's opinion, knowing he would get a candid appraisal. Jackie was always good with a shotgun, and gave Ford both barrels. He told Ressler how feeble Ford's efforts had become and how second-rate it had been made to look by the campaigns of Renault, Honda, Mercedes-Benz and Ferrari. It might not have been quite what Ressler was expecting, but it was brutally honest. 'I told Neil,' Stewart recalls, 'that Ford should quit because the fire had gone out.'

When Ressler told him that Ford was simply too deeply committed to consider quitting, Jackie advised him to rethink the entire strategy. That was when Ressler asked him if he was interested in putting together a proposal to do just that. Surprised at first, Stewart saw it as the chance to re-ignite his F1 aspirations.

He and Paul immediately began to put together 'A Proposal for Partnership', and by the end of October they were back on their way to Ford's World Headquarters in Dearborn to present it to Uncle Henry's heavy-hitters. Paul himself made a panic dash by 'The Concorde', as his father calls the world's greatest aeroplane, when other means came up short. Together with Rob Armstrong, the New Zealander whose understated ability appeared to make light work of the job of Commercial Director of PSR and who now fills the same role for Stewart GP, they made their pitch. In a move that was most unusual by the standards of sponsorship acquisition, each Ford representative had already received a copy of the proposal. That ploy, and the astonishing openness of the Stewart group, made a huge impression. Ford had perhaps become used to the take-it-or-leave-it attitude that tends to prevail in motorsport, but here was a group of businessmen laying everything out, with no hidden agendas. What Ford needed most, Jackie and Paul stressed time and again, was a 'reliable and trustworthy long-term partner in F1.' By December Ford had

You can also never get too much advice. Paul gets pearls of wisdom from Nigel Mansell, but it's all old news to Williams technical director Patrick Head. (Sutton)

one, and Stewart Grand Prix was announced officially on 4 January 1996 at the Detroit Show.

Now that the Stewarts really were heading for F1, critics suggested that Jackie ached for the limelight and was merely looking for a fresh identity, since the career that had forged his reputation now lay almost a quarter of a century behind him. He was absolutely adamant that this was not the case, and his tone was convincing. 'This is not Jackie Stewart having a play; the Ford family is too big for that. This is probably the most challenging endeavour I have ever taken on. It has been planned for some time and has come together well with the exclusive use of an engine. I know Ford's corridors, its senior management, and how it does business. But there are no delusions of grandeur on either side.'

There was an air about him of a star seeking a new challenge

The announcement of Stewart Grand Prix was a timely injection of quality. It came at a time when the obituaries of businesses such as the once-great Lotus, and newcomers Simtek and Pacific, which had succumbed to slow financial strangulation, far outweighed the births of new enterprises. F1 seemed to have become a mother that fed on her young and old alike.

Ford's decision to go with the former champion's completely untried F1 operation was bold, to say the least, and an indication of the motor giant's faith in Stewart and the strength of his proposal. But also, perhaps, the paucity of any other viable options.

The long-expected move thrust the 56-year-old Scot firmly back into the limelight. The jaunty figure had remained wholly familiar as he acted as ambassador and television commentator, and frequently could be seen ushering young royals around the paddocks of the world. And while he and Paul had set up Paul Stewart Racing, Jackie had remained intensely active in developing the handling of Ford road cars. 'I have never regretted for a single day taking the decision to retire when I did,' he would say around this time, 'even though I probably had a good few years left in me as an active driver.' Yet despite his protestations to the contrary his friends and close associates had long felt that there had been about him for some years now the air of a star seeking a bigger challenge in what was quite the busiest 'retirement' of any champion in history. With the formation of Stewart Grand Prix, that challenge had finally arrived.

Despite a full works engine deal, Jackie knew that the road ahead would be tortuous. 'It will take time and that's why the involvement is for five years,' he said. 'We thank Ford for their confidence, but we cannot deliver in five minutes.'

Paul Stewart expanded the point. 'We set our goals carefully. We didn't

Paul's personal best in F3000 came with a fighting fourth place round the streets of Pau in 1993. (Sutton)

The chance to try an F1 car came at the end of that season, just prior to Paul's retirement to focus on the business. Jackie Oliver invited him to test a Footwork Mugen-Honda at Silverstone, where the emergent Michael Schumacher was on hand to dispense advice.
(Sutton)

come in to Ford and say we were going to set the world alight right away. We had a long-term plan and that's why we've got a five-year relationship. Hopefully it will be a lot longer relationship than that. We did say we were going to learn to walk before we could run. The first two years will be very much learning years, and they will be looking for us to start performing beyond that. If people are expecting us to come in right away and start outqualifying the top four teams, that's not realistic. But we are trying to build something because sure as hell, one day, we want to challenge these people and be beating them, otherwise we wouldn't be getting involved.'

Could the Stewarts deliver at all? There were plenty of rivals prepared to voice doom and gloom predictions that they would fall flat on their faces. Said one: 'Jackie will find that being the Monday morning quarterback is a whole lot different to actually running a racing team in Formula 1. Even since 1994 the climate has changed. To keep up nowadays you just have to throw money at a project, and money is the toughest thing to find.'

Another, the founder of a highly successful F1 team, was asked when he thought Stewart's much-touted new operation might win Grands Prix, and replied cynically: 'Probably two years after his Ford contract expires.'

The more optimistic or sympathetic pointed to Jordan, and reminded others how pessimistic people were about Eddie Jordan's chances of making an impression when he entered F1 in 1991. Jordan was the talk of that season, and though 1992 almost brought the team to its knees, it subsequently recovered momentum. Again, the detractors pointed to the changed circumstances of F1 but against that had to be measured the works Ford deal, something that Jordan didn't have, and the obvious level of further funding that the major motor manufacturer had finally been persuaded to invest in its motorsport programme. There was also the unconfirmed belief

Coping with dyslexia

To watch either Jackie or Paul Stewart in action, you would never realise that either is dyslexic. Certainly, neither has ever let it stand in their way, even though Jackie was not diagnosed as being dyslexic until he was 40.

'I have to go about my business in unusual ways because of it,' Paul says, 'and I have to rely heavily on other people. Despite having a good university degree in Political Science behind me, reading and understanding the large volume of documents that come across my desk is no easy matter. I have a brief work-out each morning, to help my focus.'

Both he and Jackie work with the Scottish Dyslexia Trust, doing what they can to help other dyslexics to minimise their difficulties and acting as role models to imbue them with renewed hope and self-confidence.

that, in extremis, Ford would bail Stewart Grand Prix out if things turned really sour financially.

Though the climate of Grand Prix racing had changed beyond recognition since the early '70s, Jackie was more than shrewd enough to appreciate that. Paul Stewart Racing's activity in Formula Vauxhall, F3 and F3000 had given him and Paul hands-on experience of the climate outside F1, and though the budgets in the two feeder formulae were necessarily significantly smaller, he had strong awareness of the role of money. If Stirling Moss was the first racing driver to make big bucks, Stewart was the first to make even more once he had retired. That basic Scottish acumen had not deserted him since he gave up the cockpit and steering wheel, and he had kept firmly in touch with the current scene. If it was suggested to him that in his day only engines and chassis mattered, whereas now you needed to add a massive budget to those basics, the response was immediate and fluent.

'The single most important element is the financial structure,' he stressed whenever the question was raised. 'The companies involved will be multinational and we will be "networking" – using large companies which need each other.'

Paul made another key point. 'The important part of the relationship with Ford is that they want to be able to use us as a technical gathering point, a platform, for their engineers to see what's going on and to understand a little bit about what might be available looking further down the line. They haven't been able to do that with other teams, because they haven't been able to negotiate long-term deals. Other teams have never wanted themselves to be exposed to the possibility of being tied to a particular manufacturer which might then pull out to go to Williams, McLaren and Benetton and leave them with a whole big element of their technical knowledge and structure taken away. One of the risks that we have taken is to go on that side to try and get the company to commit properly to us. In principle we have achieved that and Ford has embraced that.

'If you ask why we have come in now, there are different elements to it. If you look at what inspires my father and what inspires me, it's slightly different. We are at different ages and different points in our careers. From my own point of view it's pretty clearcut, really. For a 30-year-old to have this opportunity is one that comes along only once in a lifetime in this fashion. I have yet to fully prove myself, so taking on such a programme in an environment that's as competitive as Formula 1 will become the major focus of my life. If you were to look at an overall picture, either I will have made it or won't have made it, based on this. This is what will dictate how I lead the rest of my life. I really want to embrace this challenge.

'Now from my father's perspective, clearly the motives are different. But he has never ceased to be an ambitious individual, which is unique in somebody who has achieved so much and kept such a high energy level. He enjoys challenges. The ingredients are right there and it makes sense.'

They were ready for the challenge.

Chapter 3

The money game

As Stewart Grand Prix's plans gathered momentum, Paul explained the roles that he and his father would each now play.

'The main focus for my father is getting the sponsors in. I'm also involved with that because of the preparation that's necessary, but he is full steam ahead on that and concentrated completely on it. I am also working with the team, pulling things together on the design side, getting the workshop set up, getting the computer equipment in, all the administrative side.'

The plan called for the F1 team to be set up and become operational in 1996 and initially to run from or near PSR's existing base in Milton Keynes, before transferring to a purpose-built factory nearby in 1998. A year after that all construction work would be taken in-house as the team became fully self-supporting. Former Brabham manager David Stubbs, a long-time PSR asset, would be senior team manager, with

faithful F3 team manager Andy Miller handling the tricky technical liaison and interface with Ford. This clearly would be a key element, as Jordan came to appreciate in 1996 when Jacky Eackelart was appointed as go-between by Peugeot.

Though there were 12 months before the Stewart-Ford's first race, that was nothing by F1 standards, and it would be a frantically tight schedule for a group of people learning how to work and interact together to get the prototype car designed, built and tested. They planned to start testing by November 1996, though Paul added: 'This will finally be decided taking into account the balance of taking extra time over research and development, versus the need to know the car intimately from our testing prior to the first race.'

The arrival of Stewart GP appeared to be nothing but a boost for the sport's profile via the status and charisma of its chairman. On the face of it, it was precisely the sort of team that the FIA wanted to encourage ever since the celebrated affair of Andrea Sassetti. This dark Italian's lamentably uncompetitive Andrea Moda team had been nothing short of an embarrassment in 1992, the more so when he had tried to secure an injunction against Bernie Ecclestone at Monza when he found that his team had finally outlasted its limited welcome to F1 paddocks. Since then the FIA had demanded financial guarantees to ensure that such nonsense could not occur again. Stewart Grand Prix was clearly such a blue chip organisation that Bernie and FIA president Max Mosley should have been salivating.

The Stewarts had already been working tirelessly to source the budget that would be required, an estimated minimum of £25 million, from commercial sponsorship. What complicated the matter was that Jackie Stewart had no intention of going the tobacco sponsorship route if he could possibly avoid it, 'because I wanted to present absolutely the right image, not just to the outside world, but also to other potential sponsors.' If anybody had the connections and the nous to achieve that, he had.

'If I go to address the Young Presidents' Club and do a 45-minute speech whose core is motorsport and the industry,' he said, 'I've probably got in that one room the best part of 400 of the biggest businesses in the world. And if one of those Young Presidents thinks that motorsport might be worth

Jackie's links with Ford still extended to regular circuit testing of the product. Here he tries the Escort Cosworth at Silverstone. (Sutton)

David Stubbs, left, with Rubens Barrichello, his mother and father and future wife Sylvana, returned to F1 with Stewart GP. Team manager for PSR's F3000 effort, 'Stubbsie' had previously overseen Brabham's F1 efforts in the late 1980s and early '90s. (Sutton)

looking into, that's 0.25 of a per cent, and I've achieved something for motor racing.'

The Ford name undoubtedly gave the Stewarts a fabulous calling card. Yet as they sought the commercial backing for their venture Jackie and Paul were to be staggered many times by just how many companies failed to recognise the potential benefits of a networking system that seemed guaranteed to boost their revenues and image.

Both Jackie and Paul invested massive personal commitment at this stage, and the tangible evidence was in the former's decision to move back to England. Back in the early days of his F1 campaign with Ken Tyrrell he had emigrated to Switzerland, buying the house that he came to adore and that represented his family home. Now it was rented out, to old friend Phil Collins. 'I had to do that,' Stewart admitted, 'because otherwise I would have been tempted to commute. It's a lovely house, it's got everything I want. Helen and I first went there in March 1968. But what are you going to do? Are you going to keep the dogs there? If the swimming pool's there, you'll go back. I know I'd just nip back for a couple of days if I could. But I've got to keep an eye on this ball.'

He moved initially to Sunningdale, within easy reach of SGP's premises, but by 1999 had moved into a new house at Buckler's Cross, near Wendover.

On the Saturday of the 1996 British

This was the prize that the 'Proposal for Partnership' had won for the Stewarts in 1997, the chain-driven version of the Ford Zetec-R V10 F1 engine. (Sutton)

GP at Silverstone, as the F1 cars prepared to go out for qualifying and as 70 seats under Paul Stewart Racing's opulent awning were being readied for occupation by corporate diners, Jackie found time to talk. Some say that he never stops. He was having what his aides called a 'wall-to-wall' day, yet it was typical that he either found, or made, time to discuss the bold new alliance with Ford that would propel him back into F1 as a team owner. The ball was rolling fast, and wind tunnel tests were already under way on the new challenger that would bear such a famous name.

He also made confident sounds about finance. 'I think our funding will be completely in place in…' a small pause. 'Three weeks. For five years.'

Sceptics might have smiled, but Stewart has never been a man given to mendacity, nor does he kid himself. 'Things have probably come together in the last five or six weeks. You couldn't have expected it any earlier. But listen, I'm not counting eggs before they've hatched. The ink's got to be dry and the cheque in the bank. But under the circumstances, I must say we are very pleased to be where we are at the moment. Now, we may get a few bad surprises, who knows, but I don't think so. The companies that we are really deeply into final issues with are all tremendously good.'

Stewart's biggest asset is his ability to reach the men who make the decisions, rather than the middlemen who like to portray that image. 'I probably have a better advantage in that respect than anybody in racing,' he agreed. But

Alan Jenkins:
a touch of Scouse

When Jackie and Paul Stewart began seeking a technical director for Stewart Grand Prix late in 1995, 48-year-old Alan Jenkins was a natural choice.

As a Liverpudlian art graduate, Jenks's passion for motorsport had already been ignited in the days when his father had taken him to watch Stirling Moss racing, and later he discovered the pleasure that he derived from designing. 'You could say that I was into designing before I could draw,' he admits.

His path into active work within the sport began when he sketched things for cars as his means of externalising his feelings. He had some friends who were involved in racing, and on one of his periodic trips to foreign races – this time to Monaco – one of them who worked as an engineer for Lotus put him in touch with Hector Rebaque. The Mexican driver was about to start racing a brace of ex-works Lotus 78s. Before long Jenks found himself part of Rebaque's team racing in the Brazilian GP.

'My first job was to design the

Alan Jenkins is entitled to look quietly exhausted after the effort that went into creating the Stewart SF-1, and the infrastructure of the new team's design department. (Formula One Pictures)

company's letterhead! When the cars arrived from Lotus there were bits missing here and there, so I set to work to draw things like brackets that were small but pretty essential!'

Later he moved on to a senior race engineering role at McLaren, where he worked with John Watson, Alain Prost and John Barnard in the early 1980s as the team prepared to swing into the steamroller mode that characterised much of the decade. In 1984 he moved across the Atlantic to take up the post of chief designer at Penske Racing, and a year later he watched Danny Sullivan's famous 'spin-and-win' triumph for the team in the Indianapolis 500.

The lure of F1 brought him to Mike Earle's Onyx team in 1987, and there he created the car that would finally race in 1989 after a season's delay due to financial shortfalls. The Onyx was good enough to take the team beyond mandatory prequalifying by mid-season, and with it the Swede Stefan Johansson took an excellent third place in the Portuguese GP.

This vital experience of working at both the top level and in building new teams was what so attracted the Stewarts, who persuaded him to quit his job as technical director for the Arrows (Footwork) team.

'I worked through the Ron Dennis renewal of McLaren,' Jenkins said, 'and I helped Penske as a car constructor, then I was one of the people who started Onyx from scratch. It was all pretty good background for the set-up of Stewart Grand Prix.'

with a fine sense of proportion he added: 'Within our little world and culture we know who the players are, but I've always had to remind myself – even after the first two World Championships – that people I sit next to at dinner parties don't necessarily know what I do. I was at a dinner party the other night in London, and there were only two people at a table of ten who even knew I was thinking of starting a Grand Prix team. It's the world of fairly big players, so you'd be rather naive if you thought you were important. They bring you down to earth, because to them it's so insignificant.'

Before long the Stewart camp began to buzz as the guests arrived and started to tuck in before watching the action from the Stewart suite, where the Hunting Stewart tartan carpeting had been laid specially. It might not yet have penetrated the hallowed walls of the F1 paddock, but the operation bore impressive hallmarks of smoothness. 'We might disappoint a few people who have unrealistic expectations next year,' Stewart observed, 'so we must be very good off-track.' That side of things was clearly already up to competitive speed.

In September he was finally able to reveal the identity of one of his sponsors. He had used his and Ford's connections to obtain a meeting with the Hong Kong & Shanghai Banking Corporation, and eventually a deal had been agreed for £25 million over five years. It was a major coup, for it gave Stewart GP its second blue chip investor.

Throughout the presentations that they made around the world, they were aided significantly by the work of Mark

Stewart, Jackie and Helen's younger son. While Paul had been infected with the motorsport virus, Mark had struck off on his own and become an accomplished film producer. His moving film material was a key part of his father and brother's commercial armoury.

Later Sanyo and the Malaysian government would also come aboard, and Stewart explained his thinking when the new car was launched. 'We have to have blue-chip multi-national companies such as HSBC, Sanyo, Bridgestone, Texaco and the government of Malaysia,' he said, 'to be able to afford this kind of budget.

'Ford Motor Company has probably contributed more than anybody else,' he continued, 'but to put an F1 team together, with all of the start-up costs, and in competitive fashion, does take money. But I don't really think of that as pressure.'

But pressure had indeed come only days after the HSBC deal had been made public. Jackie and Paul had been talking to a major company prepared to invest £60 million as the title sponsor. It had made them an offer, but now suddenly it was withdrawn, leaving them massively underfunded. Unconfirmed rumour identifies the company as British Airways, where Jackie was said to have shaken on the deal with Lord King only to have it vetoed after a change of management.

Part of the response was to re-open talks with the Malaysians. Stewart GP would not be the national F1 team as originally planned, but a deal was struck whereby they would bear allegiance via Visit Malaysia logos on the rear wings.

Home sweet home. This is the house in Nyon that the Stewarts turned their back on in 1996 in order to concentrate on business in the UK. Note that even in the 1960s the cars were Fords... (Sutton)

Preparing to climb the new mountain together, Helen and Jackie, together with their Norfolk terrier 'Boss'. (Sutton)

Then came what they still remember as Black Friday, a day on which several key decisions were expected. Every one of them proved to be negative. The project was suddenly on a knife-edge. They simply had to absorb the blows and keep the momentum rolling, while simultaneously maintaining the morale in a workforce that was suddenly beginning to wonder if it had made the right decision to join in the first place.

What lent even greater interest to the emergence of Stewart Grand Prix was the rebirth of the Ligier team, where fellow World Champion Alain Prost was to take control for the 1997 season. Both Stewart and Prost had forged their reputations from their uncanny talent for taking corners faster than anyone else, and between them they had amassed seven world titles and 78 Grands Prix victories –

split 3/27 and 4/51 between Jackie and Alain. What each proposed to do was certainly nothing new. Racing drivers had put their names to cars as constructors since the year dot. Stewart's old rivals Jack Brabham, Bruce McLaren, Dan Gurney, John Surtees and Graham Hill had all given it a go with varying levels of success, while less memorable had been the efforts of Chris Amon, Arturo Merzario and Hector Rebaque. But it was rare for two men of such remarkably similar calibre to enter F1 with their own teams simultaneously. Now each was focused on moving as fast as possible in a straight line to achieve their new business goals as team owners.

What added spice to their first meeting as F1 competitors was that each had tackled the business in a markedly different manner from the other. Prost had bought into an existing set-up; having considered that, Stewart was deliberately starting from scratch. 'We wanted,' he stressed, 'to start something that had no baggage, no compromises. We wanted this to be a new piece of paper all the way through. Paul and I are the sole partners. We make all the decisions, and we can make them quickly.'

Both Stewart and Prost were fit for their age, and would need to be. Stewart was nearing 58, yet retained the famous 'spring-heeled' gait that had been as much a trademark in his racing days as the Beatles cap, the shoulder-length hair and the big dark glasses. Prost could trim a few years off his 42 and get away with it, and was so fit that he could actually out-cycle his secondary business partner Laurent

Fignon, the one-time Tour de France star. Both soon found that they were far busier than they had ever been as drivers.

Stewart had always been financially astute, right from his early decision not to accept that £10,000 from Ken Tyrrell in return for a lifelong contract. He was better off for it in the long run. Such acumen and self-awareness lay at the heart of Paul Stewart Racing's successes, and now he used it again to clear the decks as Stewart Grand Prix moved forward. Ford had been the first partner, then came Bridgestone. The Japanese tyre giant had long been keen to challenge Goodyear's monopoly of F1, and as one of its roving ambassadors and tyre testers, Stewart was the logical first choice as Bridgestone prepared for a 1997 debut.

Prost, meanwhile, had been frus-

Jackie Stewart in 1996: businessman and team owner with some of his trophies. (Formula One Pictures)

The view a lot of company chairmen got to see in 1996: an animated Stewart goes on the financial warpath. (Sutton)

Was Ford such a good choice?

While Jackie and Paul Stewart were delighted to have signed their five-year deal with Ford, which became active in 1996, pit-lane cynics wondered just how beneficial the deal was likely to turn out. If you listened long enough to either Sauber or Minardi in 1996, you would hear a similar story. At Sauber, Heinz-Harald Frentzen and Johnny Herbert regularly bemoaned the lack of horsepower from Ford's Zetec R V10 engine. Giancarlo Minardi pulled no punches, regularly criticising the quality of the ED V8 engines he received as a paying customer, and *their* lack of horsepower. For 1997 he regrouped around Brian Hart's V8.

So Ford hadn't looked remotely like winning a race since that surprise success of 1994, and cynics had no doubts whatsoever that further problems would not be excused by Jackie Stewart. The Scot might do his tough talking behind closed doors, but he has a legendary reputation for expecting excellence in his partners.

All of this focused attention on Cosworth Engineering, the third party that had traditionally built all of Ford's F1 engines since the famous and brilliantly successful Ford Cosworth DFV of 1967. This was the engine with which Stewart had won his three world titles.

Cosworth's F1 Programme Director, Nick Hayes, was happy that they had the configuration of engine right. 'Looking at the possibilities,' he said, 'we were right in doing a V8 for 1994. And equally we were right to do a V10 since refuelling came in.' But the lack of success had prompted the subsidiary company, Cosworth Racing Engines, which made the F1 power units, to carry out a candid re-evaluation of its situation. Halfway through the previous season, Dick Scammell, a veteran from his days as mechanic to Jim Clark at Lotus, was succeeded by Brian Dickie as Managing Director. And over the winter Martyn Walters, the father of the V10, had moved to concentrate on the manufacturing side as Chief Engineer. Hayes took over his role of F1 Programme Director. But the company retained its commercial base by selling V8s to customers. Dickie explained why, when Ferrari, Renault, Mercedes-Benz and Peugeot were making do quite happily with only one engine and one customer. 'A large part of our business is building F1 engines. Naturally, on the works team level that must reflect the state of the art, hence the V10. But Cosworth is also sympathetic to the demand for customer engines, and to the need for them to be affordable by teams entering F1.'

The Stewarts did not agree.

trated initially when he tried to acquire Ligier in 1992. Following his retirement at the end of 1993 he started talks again, only to be thwarted a second time. He went back to McLaren for a while as a consultant, as the irascible Guy Ligier sold up to Benetton's Flavio Briatore. Eventually, Flavio sold again, to Alain.

After all the planning, Jackie Stewart prepares to unveil the Stewart SF-1 at London's Marriott Hotel in December 1996. (Formula One Pictures)

If the Stewarts were initially cautious on matters such as driver choice, there was some very far-sighted thinking going on in the background as the team's first challenger began to take shape early in March 1996. The man in charge not just of creating it, but also of creating the design and manufacturing infrastructure, was Alan Jenkins, a sharp designer whose past employment had included spells with McLaren, Penske, Onyx and Arrows. Paul Stewart already knew Jenkins reasonably well, having met him while testing an F1 car for Jackie Oliver's team back in 1993. They had hit it off straight away. Some time during 1995 he was lured into the new team as technical director. 'I had a good brief,' Jenkins recalls with his trademark wry smile. 'Neither Jackie nor Paul put any real limitations on

the mistakes that a glut of money can often inspire. They were all aware that they were part of something new, and if necessary were prepared to do more than their fair share in the knowledge that once they got the thing right and the successes came, the money would be there to hire more staff. A corollary of all this was that during the first year, while the team was still operating out of premises close to PSR's facilities in Milton Keynes and things were still tight, Jenks had to find suppliers of suitable quality. It was just the way Eddie Jordan had been obliged to do things back at the turn of the decade. The years of in-house manufacture were at this stage a long way off. But there was one key difference; where Jordan had its first monocoques built by specialist suppliers, Jenkins insisted that the SF-1 tubs should be built on the premises. 'It was the only way to ensure the quality we wanted, and to retain the flexibility that you need with a new design,' he explained.

what I could produce, so long as we had two cars ready to race in Melbourne in March 1997. That meant I could pretty much do what I fancied.'

The money to fund all this was necessarily limited, though better than that of some other teams, and Jenkins focused primarily on hiring the best design staff and race car manufacturing staff that he could afford. It was in a way the best situation, for it avoided

Jenkins had more than enough experience to draw a competitive car, and had done so by the end of that first month. And he was smart enough to appreciate that the aerodynamics were the most important aspect of it.

This was a period in F1 design when wind tunnel testing was becoming ever more sophisticated, but neither Ferrari nor Benetton had yet developed the full-size tunnels they would employ by the end of the century. Most teams still made do with facilities designed for 30

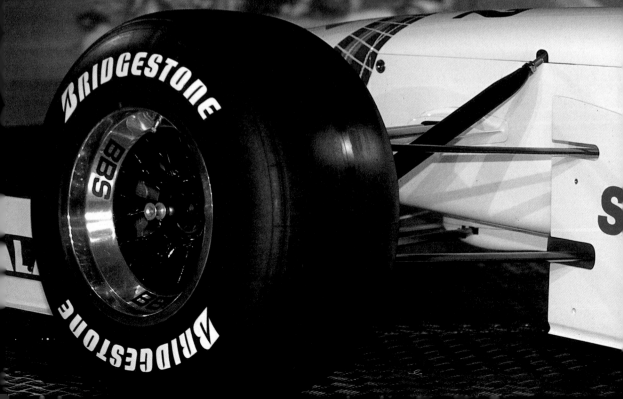

The great moment arrives. Paul, recovered from his moment of emotion, prepares to assist his father in removing the Racing Stewart tartan wraps from their SF-1. (Formula One Pictures)

It's all in the detail. The Stewart logo adorns the tiny steering wheel. (Sutton)

It didn't look it, but the Sanyo and Texaco Havoline stickers were barely dry. Commercial director Rob Armstrong only got permission to go ahead minutes before the SF-1 was revealed. (Formula One Pictures)

Not everything about the SF-1 was open for public inspection. Aerodynamicist Egbhal Hamidy preferred to keep details of the diffuser under cover. (Sutton)

per cent scale models, but Jenkins and aerodynamicist Egbhal Hamidy stole a march by doing a deal with Dave Burns's Swift racing car manufacturing company in Ste Clemente, California, where Swift had a 50 per cent tunnel. Only Williams, who has also used it at one stage, had anything as good. Tests began there on 1 July, and this bit of astute strategic thinking, and the time and effort expended there in 1996 by the SGP design team, would reap significant dividends in the long term.

As the main shape of the Stewart SF-1 began to be finalised, SGP agreed terms for Xtrac to build the six-speed longitudinal gearbox, one of the components with the longest lead time. From June the recruitment began in earnest as the Stewarts began to attract their first F1 staff, the drawing-office men, fabricators, composites experts and all the myriad individuals who help to create the world's fastest racing cars.

Chasing horses

Priority development resources at Cosworth were allocated to the V10, which F1 Programme Director Nick Hayes and his team had modified significantly since 1996. 'Over the winter we have concentrated nearly everything on performance,' he said, 'which means peak power and the shape and width of the power curve. We've gone for a lot of work on top-end power and the power curve. Quite a lot of the engine's mechanicals are new. It still revs to 16,500rpm, and we will qualify and race at that.'

He was optimistic that Cosworth would be in a better position to bring upgrades on line faster in 1997 than it could in the past, as a direct product of significantly greater – and long overdue – commitment from Ford to its F1 effort.

'The truth of it is that we have a lot more resources to play with, so we can do a lot more. We are talking now,' he said before the season had actually begun, 'about what changes we will be bringing on stream for Brazil at the end of March. Even that is a movement for us, because before we never had that sort of resource. Ford is committed much more, but not just because of Jackie Stewart's involvement. To be fair, I think Ford decided in any case that it wanted to do it properly, and went off to find the right team. We have more resources here as a result, but also Ford itself is putting a lot more into it. It has a lot of manpower working on programmes specifically for us.'

Hayes acknowledged that some of the criticism in 1996 was justified, but preferred to qualify it. 'I think at the beginning of the year the engine was very difficult as far as driveability was concerned, and it was also a fair way behind on top-end power too, so yes, that criticism was justified. But I think it was far less so as the year went on.

'Drivers always say they lack horse-power, they always will, and I don't blame them. But I think we caught up a lot during the season, and we've caught up further during the winter.'

How much remained to be seen.

The Stewarts: Victoria, Paul, Jackie, Helen and Mark pose for the cameras, but Paul's son Dylan seems less than impressed. Perhaps he just wondered why the engine wouldn't fire up. (Formula One Pictures)

The first chassis was completed by the end of August, a fantastic achievement for a team of people doing the work together for the first time, and there was another significant milestone when it passed its first mandatory crash tests that same month.

Ken Tyrrell watched the Stewarts' progress with avuncular interest. His greatest successes had come with Jackie at the wheel, and not surprisingly Uncle Ken continued to speak highly of him. 'Ever since Jackie retired from active driving he's been successful in running his own business, which has been Jackie Stewart. As a public relations man he has been second to none. Now he's into something quite different, the practical problem of actually running a company. We have to wait and see how that will work out. But I'm sure he has gathered the right people round him, and I'm sure he will be successful.

'I think he has very good connections, and his reputation as a straightforward person will stand him in good stead. Everyone knows he is an honest person, and that what he says he is going to do, he will do or will certainly attempt to do.'

But Briatore, who knew the business

The sleekness of the first Stewart racing car was all too evident, together with the superb attention to detail. (Formula One Pictures)

inside out after running Benetton since 1989, had words of caution for any aspiring newcomers. 'The crucial point is to make sure it is well funded, because without that it's not gonna work and for sure you will be going nowhere. There are only three or four teams progressing, because it costs so much money.' If that was taken as a definition of what success in F1 took, Stewart and Prost seemed well positioned in that department, too. Their biggest mutual asset was the ability to reach the men who make the decisions in multi-national companies, but Jackie was more at ease with the captains of industry than Alain.

When the project was first announced late in 1995 it was far, far too soon to speak of drivers, but the Stewarts planned to start monitoring the market from mid-season. 'We'll be looking for a driver with good experience in Formula 1, who can help us develop the team, and a younger driver as well,' Paul said, adding: 'Ideally, the latter would come from our Staircase of Talent, either from the past or the present, but realistically from the past.'

Though the F1 project would naturally take precedence as far as Jackie and Paul's time was concerned, PSR would remain involved in F3 and Formula Vauxhall, and Paul refused to rule out altogether a return to F3000 in the future to maintain the integrity of the Staircase.

Nearer the time, Jackie expanded on what he was looking for in a driver, as

It's time for drivers Jan Magnussen and Rubens Barrichello to show off their suits. (Formula One Pictures)

the media played the game of identifying likely candidates. The favourites were Brazilian Gil de Ferran, at that time starring in IndyCars, and Dane Jan Magnussen, who was at that time McLaren's F1 test driver. Both were former Paul Stewart Racing champions in F3. The fact that both were F1 rookies didn't necessarily deter Stewart.

Puppies need training, and sometimes they pee on the carpet

'The more we think about it the more we see that it's not absolutely necessary to have an established foot in the shoe. What we've really got to look at is years three, four and five, and we've got to be very sure that whoever we take on now is going to be capable of delivering then. But it may then be that we have to buy in the current man, because what we would be dealing with if we took on drivers who are new to the business, would be puppies. And puppies need training, and sometimes they pee on the carpet. You think you've trained them but they return to the same habit, occasionally. So we have to think that our puppies would become trained labradors, and not only see the object they've got to pick up but, if they haven't seen it, have a nose on them so sharp that they could find it. And they will need the discipline always to bring it back, no matter what they have to go through.' The continence of de Ferran and Magnussen, it

might be added, had rarely been called into question...

As an established entity Prost Grand Prix was in a better short-term position to sign a top-line driver, but suddenly late in 1996 the chance came for Stewart to sign up the reigning World Champion, Damon Hill.

For the latter part of the season in which he clinched his World Championship, the Englishman knew that his days at Williams were numbered, for Frank Williams and technical director Patrick Head had already taken the decision before his latest run of success to replace him with Frentzen for 1997. This was based on Hill's disappointing season in 1995. So he was on the market, looking for a drive. His options were Jordan, which was beginning to emerge as a strong contender, Arrows, which was under the new and forceful management of Scot Tom Walkinshaw – and Stewart. Naturally, Hill talked to all three parties, for F1 drivers are nothing if not thorough, but in the end he opted for Arrows prior to joining Jordan for 1998. Stewart was not disappointed, and explained why. 'We couldn't say we are disappointed that Damon won't be coming,' he said, 'because we really didn't expect him to come in the first place. It would almost have been too much. The reigning World Champion...

'If we had had Damon there would have been more pressure on the mechanics and engineers, and on the structure of a very young team. Stewart Grand Prix is like a very young child. The bones are not really fully set or grown yet. It would have been wrong for us.'

Paul and Jackie celebrate their deal with Ford's Albert Caspers, seated (below) in Jackie's 1971 Championship-winning Tyrrell 003 at the Autosports Show in Birmingham early in 1997, when the public had its first chance to view the Stewart SF-1. (Sutton/Formula One Pictures)

The less astute might not have seen it that way, but Stewart was right.

The Stewart-Ford SF-1 was launched at the Marriott Hotel in London's Grosvenor Square on 10 December 1996, and the full Stewart clan was there: Jackie and Helen, Mark, and Paul and his wife Victoria (who was pregnant with their second son Lucas) and their first, two year-old Dylan. It was their big day, but though things appeared calm and organised on the surface, behind the scenes there was controlled panic. The car was not finished until 5 o'clock that morning, and even by 10 o'clock Armstrong was still chasing permission from Sanyo and Texaco to use their logos on its elegant white flanks. This was finally granted at the 11th hour.

Ford's Martin Whitaker made an uncompromising speech outlining the company's ambitious programme to take the World Championship with Stewart, to which Jackie responded with his usual amusing banter in which he described his return to F1 as 'the most daunting challenge I have ever faced'. But it was Paul who most affected those who had joined the Stewarts to wish them well. Paul was more nervous than he had seemed all those years ago at the Carphone Group Formula Ford launch, but after all this was the biggest moment of his career. As he paid tribute to his father Paul's emotions overcame him and for a moment he was unable to continue; it was a touching confirmation of the closeness of their relationship that moved many who were there. A while later, after gathering himself, Paul added: 'From the bottom of my heart I would like to thank my father for this tremendous opportunity.'

As they unveiled the latest member of their family, father and son embraced.

The Stewarts have always been close-knit. They embrace and kiss publicly with a lack of self-consciousness or affectation that cuts right through the traditional cynicism of the F1 milieu, and is another reason why they and their team are so popular; while doing extraordinary things they nevertheless remain real people. Their team is not mired in the hyperbole and mendacity that is so often a means to flatter and fool. With the Stewarts, as with Stewart GP, what you see is what you get.

A little later at the launch, Jackie said: 'You know, I've seen all this before. But it is new to Paul. He has been under pressure for so long, and he has done extremely well to carry it off so well. I know how tough it is, believe me. And I also know that without him I could not have done this.'

Paternal pride glowed strongly that day.

Chapter 4

In the deep end

Jackie Stewart was adamant from the start that his expectations of his first season as a Grand Prix constructor were modest. 'Upper midfield, in qualifying or racing, would be terrific by the end,' became something of a mantra. But given the 27 Grands Prix victories and three world titles to his name, it was inevitable that he would suffer the burden of the great expectations of others. They were always bound to exceed the reality of Stewart Grand Prix's initial ability to deliver.

The facts, simply assessed, did not favour the team. It was brand new, and though it had many highly skilled and deeply experienced people in key positions, they had yet to be forged fully into the working relationships that can so strongly influence a team's overall efficiency. Nothing exploits weaknesses quite so much as the crucible that is F1.

As newcomers, the Stewarts were not members of the Formula One Constructors' Association (FOCA) and thus did not qualify for any of the travel concessions, or for any prize money. They were minnows swimming among sharks who could not have cared less what Jackie Stewart might have achieved behind the wheel. It was up to the team to prove itself. To bite back, or to be swallowed whole.

There was not sufficient capital available to allow the setting up of a separate test team, which could beaver away while the race team was active elsewhere, then pass on valuable findings that might help the car to go quicker. The corollary of this, besides a car that was not as highly developed as some of its opposition, was that the races themselves tended to become glorified test sessions, with all that entailed in terms of potential public embarrassment. One of the more familiar sights on television screens, not just in that first season but also the second, would be Stewart-Fords grinding to smoking halts, the logos on their rear wings only visible after the haze of liberated Texaco lubricant had dispersed.

Jackie and Paul were under no illusions. But undoubtedly it was a great moment, for father and son, as the two Stewart-Fords lined up on the grid for their first race, the Australia GP in Melbourne's Albert Park in March 1997. Barrichello had done particularly well and was an impressive 11th fastest, Magnussen 19th. 'Without a doubt,' Jackie admitted, 'this is far more nerve-racking for me than it was when I was a driver. This is the toughest race of my career!'

Rubens lasted until lap 50, when his engine broke; Jan until lap 37 when his suspension did likewise. But the show was on the road, and it had not been a disgrace by any means. Stewart GP was an active F1 team.

Barrichello was again 11th fastest for his home race, at Interlagos, but lasted only 17 laps before his suspension broke; Jan got away from 20th position on the grid and lasted only as far as it took others to tangle in a race-stopping shunt. One of the victims, he missed the restart.

Rubens was also involved in a first-corner shunt next time out in Argentina, but he had started from fifth position on the grid sandwiched between the Schumacher brothers. Stewart was indeed making progress,

Estoril, February 1997, and Jan Magnussen gives the Stewart-Ford SF-1 its first serious trial against the opposition that it will face later throughout the F1 season. (Formula One Pictures)

and Rubens in particular was making excellent use of Bridgestone's tyres. In its first season the Japanese company had signed deals with Prost as well as Stewart. Olivier Panis had qualified one of Alain's cars in third place, and might have won but for mechanical problems.

Barrichello tangled with Michael Schumacher's Ferrari on that opening lap. The German was out on the spot after what some observers deemed to be an over-enthusiastic attempt to pass, but Rubens made clever use of strategy as the safety car was deployed and was able to make two pit stops for repairs without losing a lap. Sadly, the promise evaporated with a hydraulic failure after 25 laps. Jan was an unclassified 10th, his engine having broken after 67.

Imola brought similar disappoint-

ment; Rubens's engine blew up on the 33rd lap, and Jan spun off on the third. Then came Monaco.

The status of a non-FOCA team was brought home forcibly to the Stewarts when they were denied motorhome space in the already crowded paddock, and many saw this as a deliberate slight against a man who was too outspoken and too popular for the comfort of the governing body. The positioning of vehicles within the paddock is only done with the sanction of FIA Vice President of Marketing Bernie Ecclestone, arguably the sport's most powerful figure. When discussing the location of Stewart's bus some way up the cliffside in the large covered car park reserved for other teams' transporters, he was alleged to have commented: 'I don't see what Jackie is bothered about; he's closer to the

Royals he's always talking about.' In devastating style, however, the Stewarts were to have the last laugh.

Qualifying was dry and saw Barrichello line up 10th, his best starting position of the season so far; Magnussen was 19th. But the race was run in rain, and after an excellent start Rubens soon found himself hunting in the leading pack. Before long, only Michael Schumacher lay ahead. For the remainder of two nail-biting hours the white Stewart, with its Racing Stewart tartan stripes, chased the Ferrari from a respectful but nonetheless impressive distance. Here was the world's best driver in a car developed at a cost of millions of dollars, and there was a new team in only its fifth World Championship Grand Prix, scoring its first-ever points. To add to the euphoria, Jan brought his SF-1 home seventh, marking not just the first time the team had scored, but also the first finish for both its cars. It mattered not that they won nothing for their efforts.

Up and down the pit lane there was genuine pleasure for the Stewarts, who were literally beside themselves as their tears flowed. It was all simply too much for either Jackie or Paul.

'The launch of Stewart Grand Prix had been an emotional moment for me, as I paid tribute to my father,' Paul said. 'Then came Monaco, and Rubens taking our car to second place. It would not have been so satisfying if that success had come easily. We'd had a tough time bringing the team together, then Rubens had driven so well and had fought for the position. There was an incredible feeling between my father and I at the end. All I could do was grab his head and kiss and hug him! If we hadn't had the tough time, it wouldn't have been the same. It was so, so intense. It was a fantastic feeling.

'I didn't think it was possible to achieve through business that kind of euphoria about the family unit. That

Was Ford the fairy godmother?

The deal with Jackie and Paul Stewart set the Blue Oval off in a completely new direction, by Martin Whitaker's own admission. But he was more reticent when it came to admitting the true level of Ford's financial contribution to the project. Within the F1 paddocks a common belief existed that Ford was making a huge investment in Stewart, not just in setting up the team, but in guaranteeing to cover any shortfalls in sponsorship during the project's first year.

'Ford is making a financial investment in the establishment of the team, yes,' Whitaker conceded, 'and naturally the rest of the financial investment covers the engines and their development, through Cosworth. The position has always been that we would look very carefully at what is happening around the mid-year period.'

But did that mean that Ford would actually underwrite much of the 1997 programme, if it really had to?

Whitaker would merely put on his best diplomat's expression, and reply: 'I can't say any more at present.'

The concern is evident on Jackie's face as he prepares for the most daunting challenge of his life: his team's first Grand Prix. (Sutton)

usually comes with the birth of a child, not a motor race. It was a very special moment. It was such a tough ride, and none of it had come easily. We really earned our place that day.

'I think that the relationship between my father and I is reflected in the family atmosphere at Stewart Grand Prix. We've never had barriers in the family, and we don't have them in the team, either.'

After the launch of the SF-1, emotion might have been expected from Paul, perhaps. But Jackie Stewart was the man who had so deliberately formed himself into a deflated rubber ball, devoid of all emotion, during his racing days. Yet there he was, joining his son as they wept tears of joy.

'You know,' Jackie reflected months later, 'I can't account for the emotions

that day. Really I can't. When I raced I always tried to control the emotions either in victory or defeat, happiness or even death. I always had very strong control of all of these emotions. I had never been affected in the way that I was then in Monte Carlo. I don't know what it was. It wasn't even the pressure we'd been under, or anything like that. After all, we'd gone well in Argentina, our third race.

'I think it was partly to do with Paul, that it was something we had done together, and partly to do with all the aggravation of getting all the deals together. The result could easily have happened at any race track, but maybe it was the closeness of Monaco that made it so special. There we were, sitting on these wee stone blocks in the pit lane, surrounded by trees, watching

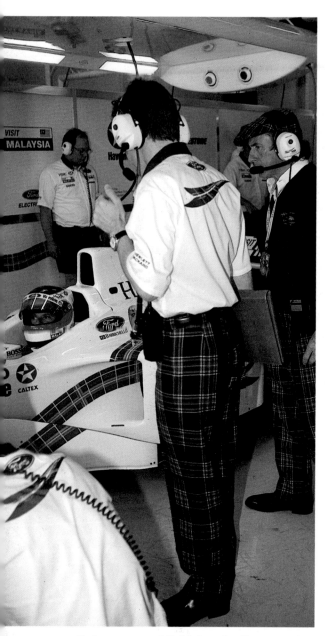

Father, son and Rubinho: the Stewarts give their driver last-minute encouragement before he qualifies the new team in 11th place on the grid in Melbourne. (Formula One Pictures)

Racing at last! Rubens ran strongly in Albert Park, until the engine broke on the 50th lap. (Formula One Pictures)

By Argentina this was a view rivals had become used to seeing. Barrichello put his SF-1 fifth on the grid in Buenos Aires. (Formula One Pictures)

a tiny television set. It was primitive almost, not like being up on a pit wall. Maybe it was the intimacy of the two of us having sat there together, rather than being separated on the pit wall…

'It just meant so much. It was an immensely important moment. And, you know, I was annoyed with myself, weeping like that. Now I just laugh and tell people it was because I had never been second at Monaco. I was third after leading in 1965; after that I either won or retired!'

Whatever else might happen over the balance of the season, nothing would ever erase the magic of that moment.

Spain brought the team down to earth with a bump, with engine failure for Barrichello, and Magnussen finishing a lowly 13th, but there was another upturn in Canada. It was a tough weekend. First Jackie received further flack for demanding that the implementation of F1's technical regulations should be carried out in a more analytical manner. Then the team fussed about seemingly endlessly before Rubens finally slipped in a highly impressive third fastest time to underline the SF-1's fundamentally excellent aerodynamics. This brought great hope for the race, but it evaporated almost immediately. The Brazilian was given a

Mayhem at the first corner, as Michael Schumacher tangles with Barrichello. (Formula One Pictures)

heavy fuel load in the hope of getting by with only one stop, and he was quickly engulfed at the start and dropped to eighth. In the first turn he clipped his front wing on the back of David Coulthard's McLaren, which upset the handling. Meanwhile Jan got tied up in another tangle, this time with Panis, and was out on the spot.

The nadir of the season came next, with the British GP

The qualifying euphoria gave way to embarrassment as Rubens lost places to the Tyrrells, with their customer Ford V8s, and the plan to make do with only one stop backfired when he received a 10-second stop-and-go penalty for passing Mika Salo under a yellow flag. Rubens had that bent wing and had also lost sixth gear, but nevertheless the Ford V10 engine's performance had now become a serious cause for concern. It was still the only engine of its kind in F1 that continued to rely on chains to drive its camshafts; the others used toothed belts that absorbed less horsepower. Worse still, the Ford was frequently unreliable. Straight after the race, two years to the event since he had first taken the momentous decision to take Ford Motor Company at its word and plunge ahead with an F1 proposal, Stewart headed back to Dearborn for some serious discussions.

Another engine failure took Barrichello out of the French GP at Magny-Cours, where Magnussen, who had led him, retired with a brake problem caused by a broken duct. The nadir of the season came next, with the British GP at Silverstone. For obvious reasons, Stewart GP desperately wanted to do well on its home soil, but qualifying was a nightmare. Barrichello's race car broke its engine, and after he had transferred to the spare, which was set up for Magnussen, it caught fire. Rubens actually qualified in Jan's car, in 21st place, with the Dane only six slots higher. In the race both came to smoking halts with broken Ford V10s. The same thing happened again in Germany and, for Rubens, in Hungary. There, Jan retired after another collision.

Magnussen was briefly a star in Belgium, where the race began in heavy rain. Rubens spun off on the ninth lap, but Jan climbed from 18th place on the grid to fourth as others made their first pit stops, running on wet-weather tyres but with chassis settings suited to a dry track. He eventually finished 12th. Monza threw up another massive disappointment. On a track where the excellent aerodynamics should have paid dividends, the cars were well off the pace.

It took the newly re-introduced Austrian GP, on the new A1 Ring, to pull the team out of its despair. It was a track particularly suited to Bridgestone's tyres, a fact demonstrated by rookie Jarno Trulli leading for a long way in a Prost. Barrichello qualified fifth and ran second to Trulli for the first 24 laps, until Jacques Villeneuve overtook him. After his final pit stop he was challenging Schumacher for

A marriage made in heaven

Rubens Barrichello was only 19 when he first drove an F1 car. Yet in the GP of Europe at Donington Park in 1993, where his compatriot and mentor Ayrton Senna starred, the young Brazilian was the day's other talking point.

A year later Barrichello survived an horrendous accident at Imola. Two days later his great friend Senna was dead. By any account Barrichello was already an extraordinarily mature 21, but the tragedy forced him to grow up even faster. 'I couldn't believe it. Really, it was a massive, massive shock. And then the funeral   I had never been through any kind of experience like that with death before. My grandfather died, but I was so young … Ayrton's was the first time that I went to a funeral. It was really difficult. Twice difficult, because when I came back to drive I had my crash and his death to get over. But when you fall off the horse you have to climb back on as quick as you can. Now, I really do think that Ayrton is an angel, and he's alongside God and he's looking after me.'

Barrichello raced again, and took his first pole position, at Spa, later that year for the Jordan team. But by 1996 the magic had gone from the relationship. When Paul and Jackie Stewart came knocking, he was ready to open the door. Their relationship clicked immediately, cemented by that extraordinary second place at Monaco, and has since gone from strength to strength as the former cham-pion and his son worked so hard to give him the right car with which to express his talents. Barrichello, who was born on the same day as his father (also Rubens) and who shares a very close relationship with him, felt relaxed in a situation where Paul and Jackie so obviously had a similar friendship.

'In Formula 1 you have to be aggressive,' is Barrichello's philosophy. 'You have to have a good car, and to be aggressive. That's all Michael Schumacher is. He has a good car and he's aggressive. And more and more I'm learning how to be that. The testing in Formula 1 is so important. As much as you do, that much you are going to learn.'

Perhaps it was no surprise that the only man who beat him in Monte Carlo was Schumacher himself.

Rubens Barrichello proved an inspired choice to lead Stewart Grand Prix into battle. (Formula One Pictures)

seventh place, moving back up the field, when he left the road and spun. Magnussen, too, was in good form, running fourth initially. Even though his engine also broke, the performance was sufficient to maintain the Dane's drive with the team. This had been in question after a string of disappointing races.

Barrichello's form continued in Luxembourg, with the race-of-convenience run on Germany's Nurburgring track. The fastest Bridgestone qualifier with ninth place on the grid, he took maximum advantage of a first-corner accident which saw Ralf Schumacher take off brother Michael, and climbed as high as third place by the 43rd lap as David Coulthard's McLaren blew up its Mercedes engine. Just as Mika Hakkinen's car performed similar hari-kari a lap later, and Barrichello was poised to move up to second place behind Villeneuve, hydraulic failure brought another promising run to a halt. Once again Magnussen kept his end up, running fifth behind Rubens until a driveshaft broke after 40 laps.

There were two races remaining, but neither left anything for Stewart. In Japan Magnussen led Barrichello until the fourth lap. Just as Rubens went by

After a brilliant performance in the rain the Brazilian and his Stewart-Ford were beaten only by the might of Ferrari and Michael Schumacher. (Formula One Pictures)

Jan lost his downforce and spun; three laps later, while chasing Damon Hill's Arrows, Rubens himself spun off. In Jerez, the scene of Michael Schumacher's ill-starred attempt to squeeze Villeneuve off the road and the French-Canadian's successful run to the World Championship, the Stewarts ran midfield until Rubens's gearbox broke. Jan was ninth.

Everyone has the right attitude, we have all invested tremendous energy

---

The first year, then, was a mixture of good and bad, of emotional highs and lows. Monaco, of course, was the peak in a season in which the newcomers had survived with honour and impressed strongly at times, although at others they had plumbed the depths.

'In the three months since June the team did not have the momentum that it was enjoying between March and June. But if we look at it overall we would have to say that after the Austrian GP the team was ahead of its expectations and that is not just saying it to make it sound good,' Jackie summarised. 'We went to Australia, the furthest possible geographic point that any GP could be from your home base, for our first race. Logistically that was not only an extraordinary expense but presented an amazing set of challenges. To qualify both cars, well, and then to have both running in the top 10 during the race, even though they did not finish, was the start of a honeymoon period. And that honeymoon only got better by our third race where we qualified fifth fastest in Argentina. That was a pretty remarkable thing.

'Sure there were disappointments; they definitely included Imola and Barcelona. But take into account second at Monaco and third on the grid in Canada with a car that hardly had any wing on it and was thus totally depending on good aerodynamics, good mechanical grip and, of course, its Bridgestone tyres, and I think it was an amazing performance. We then entered a spate of very spectacular engine failures. There was a lot of pressure to do well in front of the British crowd and we had a very disappointing Silverstone. Hungary was bad too, as we had anticipated being very competitive there.

'It was very pleasing to go to Austria and do so well, even if we came away without any points, because the car delivered from the tyre a very well-balanced package.

'I never thought qualifying mattered that much when I was driving; I used to set the car up to allow me to race the full distance. But having said that, qualifying is something we need to be better suited at next year. But on the whole both we and Bridgestone were on a learning curve, and as a team we had all the money we required to race in our first full season. At the end of it the racing team was not in overdraft,

Jumping for joy: Rubens celebrates his second place, which seems to have pleased Michael Schumacher too. (Formula One Pictures)

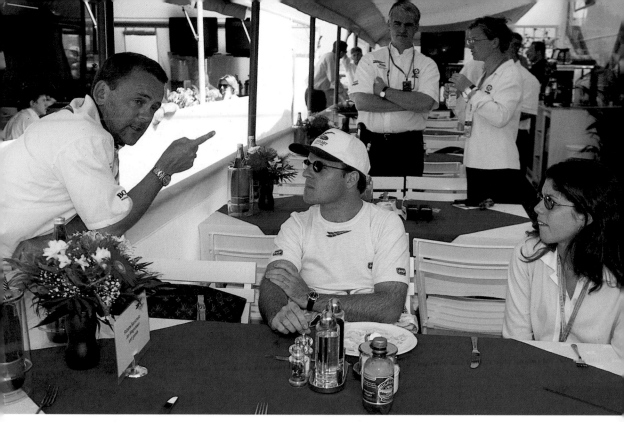

Without question Barrichello was the ideal driver for the new team, and the relationship clicked right from the start. (Formula One Pictures)

and we had a very good little car and a good bunch of people.'

That was the upside, and Stewart GP seemed a happy team by the standards of the F1 pit lane. Jackie agreed. 'If it's got a chance of being happy, this is the best chance because we are all new, and bright-eyed. I hope we never lose that, and I hope we don't ever lose our sense of humour or our friendliness. Everyone has taken the right attitude, we have all invested tremendous energy, and the level of commitment has been terrific. I have no regrets, none whatsoever.'

On the downside, however, was the lack of reliability. 'That really was the most enormous disappointment, because I believe we could have

finished in the top six more than once if we had had it. And when we were so off the pace at Monza, I really had to ask myself, "What are we doing here?" I wasn't going to accept that.'

For those who had not worked with Stewart as a driver, it was also heartening that the pressures of team ownership had not eroded his fundamental approachability. It transpired that he felt very strongly about such things. 'I wouldn't have expected to change,' he said. 'I've had experience of other businesses. And I'm at an age where you learn that you can't be over-intensive, because if you do become too intense about what you are doing you generally get over the top about all sorts of things. That leads you into

94

more trouble than you want.'

Life as a team owner had nonetheless been a real eye-opener for a man deemed by his peers to border on workaholism.

'I thought I lived quite a tough life as a driver when I was doing it,' he admitted. 'But it's a shadow in comparison with what you've got to do to have a team, run it and finance it. The infrastructure and the ramifications of the number of people or the logistics, whether travel, clothing, office space, decoration, entertaining or commercially selling – there is nothing that doesn't come through as a new problem. That infrastructure is something that never existed before. It has to be either created, or found out about.

'You get accidents, for example, and you've got to fly racing cars somewhere' – he blanched visibly – 'at a cost of £20,000! Do you do it? Because if you are going to do it, it's got to be done like that!' He snapped his fingers. 'You know, I've never ever been busier. My 18- or 19-hour days are normal, and I've been doing them now for probably 24 months. As a racing driver I was busy, make no mistake, and that was one of the reasons I retired. I was getting considerably more aggravation out of it than I was getting pleasure.'

Warming to a theme, he proceeded to outline his bygone lifestyle, and to paint a vivid perspective of the demands that face team owners in modern-day F1. 'I don't think that the current GP driver does anything close to what I did. The number of appearances I did was colossal. It was a new industry then and I was the first to be commercially taken advantage of because I had learned how to present myself.

'I was speaking to somebody the other night who had been looking at Roman Polanski's *Weekend of a*

Mixing business with business. In Magny-Cours during the French GP meeting, Jackie and the team help Ford with a spot of promotion for the new Puma road car. (Sutton)

Champion film which had been shown recently out on ITV. It reminded me that on that weekend there was a *Daily Express* readers' competition where a whole bundle of them came down to Monte Carlo. I must have had four functions: breakfast, a bus trip round the circuit with me commentating, drinks with them, dinner... People with no knowledge of motor racing at all. Apart from that we were with Elf-Acquitaine, the biggest company in France, which was on a big bandwagon using F1 as its only projection. It was using me very heavily, and so were Goodyear and Ford Motor Company.

The atmosphere was very different from when Stewart was a driver

---

'At that time I was doing something literally every day. And I was doing six or eight countries a week, sometimes five or six countries a day. And I was testing much more than they do today. We would go to Kyalami or Paul Ricard and do two Grands Prix a day for something like 18 days. In those days there really was a tyre war on, and no restriction on testing. And it wasn't just F1. I was doing CanAm at the same time. Europe one week, America the next. And the Americans knew much more than the Europeans how to make appearances dynamic. Rod Campbell was handling Liggett & Myers, who were sponsoring the L&M Lola. I would fly in and that same night do cocktails and a dinner. The next night I'd fly by private plane and we'd do a whole lot of different cities and different states. Then I'd be getting on another plane on Sunday night, flying back to Europe, and then be testing on the Tuesday or Wednesday and racing on the Friday, Saturday and Sunday. Then I'd be going back to test the CanAm car or do another set of appearances...'

In 1971 he contracted mononucleosis, and a year later a duodenal ulcer that haemorrhaged. 'Both of those things took an immense amount out of me. I'm not trying to belittle what the current guys do, but they really don't understand how heavy the load was in those days. It was a new discipline. I was making the money I was making because of that. I wasn't getting a large driving fee. That might have been £20,000. So it was a different world, and I got exhausted twice a year. Once around April, though sometimes it would drip on to late June, early July, and then in October I would get totally swamped again. Really down. And in those days I was reasonably fit, and I had a personal trainer before everyone else got started on that.'

Then came the kicker, as he added: 'But having said all that, none of it comes close to what running a team demands.'

Stewart also found that the atmosphere in the pit lane was markedly different since he had quit driving. Things were more intense, more secretive. 'You come to a Grand Prix and frankly you're in your own motorhome or garage and you don't go and visit other people. I don't really care if any

Stewarts in Stewarts

In the past Paul Stewart had driven the Tyrrell 003 that his father had taken to the World Championship in 1971, but at the end of 1997 he and Jackie marked an auspicious and historic occasion by driving their own Stewart SF-1s at Silverstone.

'I'm proud of the way we went about that day,' Paul recalls. 'I was keen to do it, with Ford's help, but from the start we insisted on having two cars for my father and myself so that the team as a whole could be properly represented. It was a terrific experience, and I was surprised how quickly things came back despite my four-year absence from a racing cockpit. Mind you, come the end of the day it was a bit like the grandparents handing back the baby!'

There's no doubt who Helen Stewart thinks is number one, as her husband and son prepare to drive their own F1 cars. There are no team orders, but Jackie and Paul give each other racing room as they make history as the only father/son team partnership to drive their own cars at Silverstone, in October 1997. (Sutton)

30 YEARS OF FORMULA ONE POWER
——— 1967–1997 ———

other team comes into our garage, but at Monza we had dinner the night before the race with some guests and wanted to get into the pit lane. We went through one of the racing teams and I said: "Would you mind terribly if we go through. Don't worry, I'll put my blinders on..." I said it as a joke. And I never noticed but the people behind me, that I was taking through, said that the team personnel certainly didn't like that. And I thought: "What the hell are they doing?" I think that's going a little too far. If we have something with technology that we want to care for, we just cover it over.' Just as key parts of the SF-1 had coyly been covered with Racing Stewart tartan at the launch.

'It's a very closed shop, and that's the culture that's been created. I don't necessarily think that's right or appropriate. Maybe it will break down, maybe we'll get like everybody else. But there are people in there who are light and amusing and a have a good sense of humour, who could make it a little more comfortable. But F1 is very constipated.

'Hey, listen, we may change. If we get highly successful maybe we'll get constipated, I don't know. But it's not just the highly successful teams that are like that! It's an arrogance, in a way, which is rather silly.'

But overall he had enjoyed himself, and like Paul was feeling comfortable with his new role. 'The nicest thing

By mid-season Ford's celebration of 30 years in F1 was sagging, and Martin Whitaker's expression was an indication of the rough patch the team was going through. (Sutton/Formula One Pictures)

about my life is that it's a whole kaleidoscope. F1 is now a very important part of it, but I still do my Ford Motor Company work and I still do my other boards and my other activities. And most of the people I mix with are considerably more successful than I am. Usually they are the best at what they do. And they don't behave with arrogance like that ...'

Overall, Rubens Barrichello had finished 13th in the 1997 World Championship for Drivers, on the strength of the six points scored at Monaco, though it was really 14th if you ignored the FIA's feeble penalty levied on Schumacher. He had been disqualified from second place overall behind Jacques Villeneuve for the

stunt he pulled on the Canadian in Jerez. Stewart-Ford was 9th out of the 10 teams that scored points in the Constructors' title chase.

Parts of Stewart Grand Prix's first season had been successful; the only problem was that there were not enough of them. Even in its first season, ninth place out of 10 in the Constructors' World Championship was not what any of the parties involved really had in mind. It was not a situation that could be tolerated for another season, but while the Stewarts set about corrective surgery for 1998, Ford had also been indulging in some more serious self-scrutiny. Its Scottish alliance was only part of a far-reaching redevelopment of its entire F1 programme, the details of which became apparent as the season progressed. That October overall control was given to Dan Davis, already a director of Ford Special Vehicle Operations in Detroit. The 48-year-old had an impressive track record within the company since joining in 1976, and was a motorsport enthusiast.

If used correctly motorsport can provide dividends year after year

'This position is as much about managing successful relationships with drivers, teams and sanctioning bodies, as it is about the technology and programmes it takes to put together a championship effort,' he said. That echoes the new-felt belief that one reason why Ford had thus far failed to deliver in F1 had its roots every bit as much in the personal side as in the technical. 'Motorsport is a very important part of Ford Motor Company's business today, and if it is used correctly both from a marketing and a technology sense, it can provide dividends to the company year after year. From my previous experience, I am convinced the technology transfer aspects of the programme are real, both

in terms of developing products and in developing young engineers.'

Martin Whitaker would be Davis's right-hand man in the European arena. He had joined Ford in 1995 as Communications Director, and midway through 1997 succeeded Australian Peter Gillitzer as Director of Ford Motorsport, Europe. A former journalist who started with *Motoring News* before moving to press relations roles at the RAC MSA, the FIA, then McLaren, Whitaker knew that the company faced a mammoth task.

One of the things guaranteed to light his fire was to mention the 'unknown' championship of 1994. 'That really was one of the best-kept secrets of all time!' he agreed. 'It riles me, because everyone talks about it that way. At that time our motorsport programme was being driven, effectively, just by our motorsport department. I was staggered when I arrived at Ford and found that there was no platform from which we viewed our European motorsport strategy. You have to take into account the various important reasons for going into motorsport from your product, marketing and communication departments – all those different elements of the overall business structure.'

His job hadn't become any easier when Peter Sauber learned that his team would not be the works Ford runner in 1997. One of Whitaker's first tasks was to tiptoe through this potential minefield as Sauber counterproposed a semi-works deal whereby his team would use engines a specification or two behind Stewart's. Ford didn't necessarily disagree with that,

No moments were ever wasted as long as Jackie had access to a tape recorder, even in the air (above), but there was still time to play hard too (below). Stewart's shooting remains as sharp as ever. (Formula One Pictures)

Rubens did more mileage on foot than in his SF-1 at Silverstone, the nadir of the season. Engine reliability had reached rock bottom. (Formula One Pictures)

but Jackie Stewart was implacably opposed to anything that might weaken the overall effort. In the end, after strenuous efforts to change Ford's mind, Sauber and partner Fritz Kaiser pulled off a remarkable deal to run Ferrari engines instead.

Whitaker perceived his toughest problem as something over which he had no control: increasing the performance of the V10. 'You rely solely on other people to do that for you. And we will stand or fall on their efforts.' But it was clear that a lot of attitudes also had to be changed, not least at Cosworth Engineering. In those days, critics suggested that Ford needed a relationship where Cosworth did more of what Ford wanted and rather less of what *it* wanted, for Cosworth had a reputation at that time of being somewhat complacent and arrogant.

'I think it's a case of developing better personal and human relationships,' Whitaker countered diplomatically. 'As a matter of priority we need to develop a better working relationship with Cosworth. The company has its reputation, and it's as much at stake as everybody else's. I think we are victims of our own success in the past, with the DFV, and that everybody expects us to come straight out of the box with a super-quick engine.

'It is essential to the overall success of our motorsport strategy that we give the sport higher profile within the company. I presume that one of the reasons why I've got the job is that I have developed very good relationships with senior management. If you're not talking with senior management, you are effectively hiding yourself in a hole.'

It seemed that, at last, Ford's management was finally prepared to bite the bullet again, and to start giving full support to its motorsport programme after years of apparent indifference. Where Honda and Renault, particularly, and latterly Mercedes-Benz, had invested heavily in engine development, Ford had appeared content to run on cruise control. But at least the noises it was now making were encouraging. Everybody began looking forward with tremendous enthusiasm to 1998, a season that would flatter only to deceive with cruel monotony.

Chapter 5

The second year is always harder...

The first cut might be the deepest, but in F1 the second season is always harder than the first. It was an axiom that Stewart Grand Prix would learn the hard way.

Setting up a team is inevitably extremely tough, but there is usually a favourable time factor that allows a degree of flexibility. There is also usually more time for planning and execution, even if it may not always seem that way to those at the epicentre of the maelstrom. But the second season comes along no matter what; the dates are finite, the scheduling definite, and all the time these factors have to be catered for while the team is already racing, and learning tough lessons that require remedial work. This need for simultaneous planning and action stretches any organisation's efficiency to breaking point.

The Stewarts knew this. Moreover, both were aware that while the Jordan team had been the talk – and to an extent the toast – of 1991, its 1992 season had been an unmitigated disaster in terms of results. But even they could not have envisaged the traumas

More confident, more aggressive, Paul Stewart outlines Stewart GP's aspirations during the 1998 launch. (Formula One Pictures)

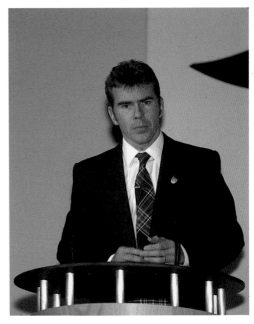

Played in by the extraordinary driving rhythms of the Scottish band Macumba, Jackie, Rubens, Jan and Paul look rather more comfortable than Jenks, who is finding the cockpit of SF-2 a tight fit. (Formula One Pictures)

that would make 1998 such a miserable experience. There was one indication that the road ahead was not smooth when the FIA publicly called into question Stewart GP's ability to meet its financial obligations for the season, and requested assurances. The team was sufficiently well-funded and proved it, and the demand was seen by many as a cheap trick to put the Stewarts in their place.

'Going into 1998 and beyond,' technical director Alan Jenkins said, 'the biggest challenge is to be a key part of the process of improving our competitive position every season, to get to the very top.

'Even though the ground plan had been laid, in 1997 it was in large part – and inevitably – new-team enthusiasm that carried the team through its first racing season. We know that in our second season we cannot count on that motivation alone.

'My aims and ambitions are many: to design a better car, to encourage the whole design team, to be the catalyst that unlocks the creativity in all the excellent people around me.

'Collectively, we are on the way to establishing ourselves as a fully fledged team: taking part competitively in all the races, building a test team, setting up a manufacturing base second to none. And that – "second to none" – would be a good motto for everything we are trying to achieve at Stewart-Ford.'

For a start, there were new regulations. These called for narrower cars that ran, for the first time since Jackie had been so instrumental in developing the slick racing tyre in 1971, on grooved dry-weather rubber. The radical change was intended to reduce grip and therefore cornering speeds, and to increase lap times. It meant that every designer had to open up a completely new avenue of research, and those who had been in a position to experiment with interim cars mid-way through 1997 would have an advantage. Stewart GP had not been in any sort of position to make such empirical experiments.

At the same time the team was to lose part of the advantage it had enjoyed in its first year. With Goodyear's withdrawal, Bridgestone had been obliged to step forward as sole supplier to F1, so that everyone would run on its tyres. It was more than likely that the company would design them around the requirements of McLaren and Ferrari rather than Stewart and Prost. Due to the monopoly situation, Bridgestone now also had far less incentive to develop new compounds and constructions, something else that had helped Stewart in 1997.

Nevertheless, the ramifications of such changes lay in the future, and when the Stewart-Ford SF-2 was unveiled at Ford's UK headquarters in Warley the message from Jackie and Paul was predictably upbeat: 1998 was to be a year of consolidation.

'Our first season was beyond our expectations,' Jackie said. 'Not just because of Monaco, but because in at least three Grands Prix we were at the front and could so easily have had podium finishes. I'm sure that, in many ways, 1998 will be more difficult. Paradoxically, because we had such a poor season of reliability in '97, people may expect too much of us in '98. It might be suggested that if only we can be reliable, then we're going to be competitive. But that would be asking

The Stewart SF-2, a new car for the new regulations. (Formula One Pictures)

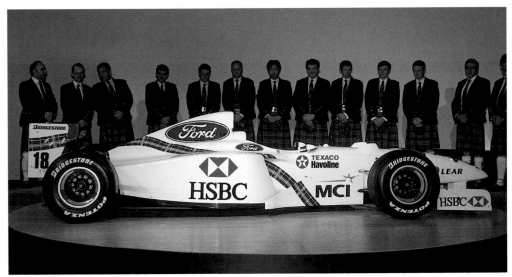

The Magnussen Affair

'Jan,' Jackie Stewart said with evident regret in his voice, 'was an enigma. We just never seemed to be able to figure out what to do to get the best out of him.'

The previous August the young Dane's tenancy of the second Stewart seat had been under threat after a series of disappointing performances. But then he had perked up and begun to demonstrate the talent that had made him stand out so much as a PSR driver in F3 back in 1994. That year he had bettered Ayrton Senna's record with 14 wins in a season, and was widely being tipped as the Brazilian's natural heir. But nothing could have been further from the truth.

In his F1 debut, for McLaren at Aida in 1995, Magnussen had, ironically, run Barrichello close, while blowing off teammate Mark Blundell. But for the majority of their partnership at Stewart, Rubens had the upper hand. Some said that Jan missed the counsel of his brother, who had acted as go-between/interpreter during his karting and F3 days; others that his enforced seasons of ITC racing with Mercedes-Benz, which followed his hyper-successful F3 season, had taught him bad ways that he could not resolve. Whatever, the problems that he experienced when practice driving a rally-tuned Ford Escort Cosworth at Oulton Park summarised his enigmatic behaviour.

According to observers, Jan would begin his day sliding the car all over the place, and it would take Stewart until the lunchbreak to calm his style down and get him on the pace. Then he would be quick. After lunch he would revert to the ragged style, and the smoothing would have to begin all over again.

'To be fair to Jan, we weren't geared up sufficiently to give him the test mileage that he needed,' Alan Jenkins admitted. But few people in the team really felt that the Dane demonstrated the hunger and commitment necessary to stay in an F1 seat. It was as if, having got to F1, he wasn't sure what was required of him.

Stewart kept him in play throughout the 17 races of 1997, though he did come close to being replaced until his performances picked up dramatically in Austria. Then he showed similar pace to Barrichello. But in his seven races in 1998, it was not until the seventh that he showed similar flair. Most of the time he just looked lacklustre. Before long he was on probation. 'I have no problem with that at all,' Paul Stewart replied in response to criticism that such a move was more likely to put Magnussen under further strain. 'Last year we gave Jan every opportunity in the first part of the season to perform with zero pressure. None whatsoever. We put more pressure on in the last third, and he performed. And then this season it has slipped away again. My response is that applying pressure is the right way to do things. It's not a question of being nasty or rude or anything, or condescending. Just being realistic about it.'

Ironically, Magnussen's first – and so far last – World Championship point came just too late to save his career.

Jan himself cited the lack of test

running, and complained that he had to do all his learning during practice and qualifying. 'The team is only capable of giving 100 per cent on one car,' he said, a comment that replacement Jos Verstappen would repeat. Jos felt that he did slightly better because he had the experience to play a marginally better game, but when he left he did so without pulling any punches, and was quoted as describing Stewart as 'the most disorganised team I have ever driven for'. In particular he cited the lack of development, and the attention he felt that Barrichello received.

In his case it was a personality clash with Jackie Stewart that undermined the relationship. That and his steadfast refusal to take part in any of Stewart's driving lessons at Oulton Park. Unlike Jan, Jos was not the sort to bite his tongue when plain speaking would do.

As for Magnussen, he drove in 24 races for the team. That was probably 20 more than any other F1 team would ever have countenanced in a sport that takes no prisoners.

'You see, Jan, the car's not mellow...' Stewart in impassioned mode with his Danish driver. By mid-season they parted company, with mutual regret. (Formula One Pictures)

At the beginning of 1998, great expectations were harboured for the new belt-driven version of Ford's Zetec-R V10. (Sutton)

too much too soon. I expect a conservative year, because we still have a lot to learn.'

Paul, who now found himself managing a company with more than 150 people and growing fast, could look back on a cathartic first season. 'The toughest task was trying to stay on top of all the issues, which are complex and varied. I was dealing, for much of the time, with people who had far more experience than I did. There were the growing pains of the team to contend with, and outside the team we had rule changes to react to, and negotiations on matters like F1's Concorde Agreement.'

At least the team became a signatory to the new Agreement for 1998, which eased its travel burden enormously while bringing other less well publicised benefits.

'I'm looking for Stewart-Ford to be consistent, and consistently good,' said Paul. 'I want to see us qualify regularly in the top 10 and finish far more races, which in turn should bring us regular points.'

The main aim was to graduate to being a top six team by season-end, and

to achieve this end Eghbal Hamidy had gone over SF-1's profile with a fine-tooth comb, refining its aerodynamic shape, while Alan Jenkins had taken a fresh look at virtually every area. In the end, the only major items carried over from the old car to the new were wheel/axle assemblies and some steering components.

The aero programme had been initiated as early as the week after the team's debut in Australia in 1997, and had remained ongoing, for the narrow track and grooved tyre regulations had far-reaching repercussions as far as airflow was concerned. By mid-June Jenkins had come to appreciate the need for a change to the car's fundamental characteristics and the layout of the engine. Drawing fully on the growing strength of the relationship between the team, Ford and Cosworth, he was able to take some significant steps in amalgamating the package of engine, chassis and aerodynamics.

'While an overall reduction from 200 to 180 centimetres may not sound much,' he explained, 'that 10 per cent correlates to a loss of up to 30 per cent of the air-space available between the wheels and the structure of the car. That clearly has a knock-on effect on airflow, both externally in the way it affects performance of such areas as the rear diffuser, and internally in terms of cooling.'

I promised the team we would never be in this position again

While Stewart GP recreated its car, Ford came up with an all-new engine that relocated the oil pump and tanking, and for the first time relied on belt-drive for the camshafts. These changes enabled Jenkins to integrate the engine far more efficiently from the aerodynamic point of view, and far more use had been made of Ford's massive facilities. Testing on kinetics and compliance rigs in Dearborn, and four-poster rig work in Dunton, went hand-in-hand with the work carried out by SGP-based Ford Vehicle Dynamics engineers who created the carbon fibre front suspension, a multi-link rear suspension, and the torsion bar springing. They were also instrumental in the creation of the car's major technical change: the advanced carbon fibre gearbox casing.

So there was great enthusiasm for the Stewart-Ford SF-2; the only problem was that it was dramatically late. So late, in fact, that the team was still completing its brace of cars when it arrived in Melbourne for the first race. They were literally finished at the 11th

hour, after team personnel worked ridiculous hours into each night. There and then Jackie made them all a solemn promise: 'I promised them that we would never be in the same position again,' he said. 'It was just not acceptable.'

Nor was the performance Down Under. Barrichello qualified 14th but never left the grid as his gearbox failed at the start. To compound the disaster, Magnussen went for a gap that didn't exist while challenging Ralf Schumacher on the second lap, and went off the road. The South American races saw a 10th place finish apiece for Jan and Rubens, and two transmission failures. But if the on-track performance was disappointing, it was nothing compared to the heat being generated by the mutual dissatisfaction with the situation of Stewart and Ford.

This first seeped into the public arena at Imola, where pressure was mounting from Ford. In 1997 both Jackie and Paul had been extraordinarily reluctant to voice the remotest criticism of Ford's exploding V10, either in public or off the record, and had stoically reiterated the mantra that Ford would get it right. But now many of Ford's and Cosworth's representatives did not seem to feel bound by the same code of honour, and round Ford's motorhome in the paddock it was not difficult to find critical voices inferring that the Stewarts were not up to the

No matter how closely Jenkins and Barrichello worked in Brazil, there was no disguising the fact that the team was in trouble. (Formula One Pictures)

The San Marino GP at Imola was a disaster that compounded off-track disquiet among certain Ford personnel. (Formula One Pictures)

job. Some appeared to have forgotten all about the five-year contract. It was a tough time for all concerned.

It wasn't helped by rumours that Ford was considering switching to the Jaguar brand. While the Stewart-Ford tag had a ring to it, sceptics doubted that Jaguar would want anything but Jaguar in the title, and the mill began

churning out stories to the effect that Ford would shortly be buying the Stewarts out of the team they had created. There were also suggestions of secret talks with Benetton.

To make matters worse still, the race was another disaster. At the start Jan walloped Rubens up the back, forcing him into retirement, then he himself

quit eight laps later with another gear-box failure. Spain brought some welcome relief when Rubens qualified ninth, made a brilliant start, and kept World Champion Jacques Villeneuve and Johnny Herbert behind him all the way to the flag, to take an honourable fifth place.

This upswing generated tremendous expectation for Monaco, after the 1997 run, but there was nothing but further disappointment as both cars broke

their suspension after relatively undistinguished runs.

This was a topsy-turvy season, however, and there was another bright patch in Canada as Rubens led Jan home, the duo finishing fifth and sixth. This was the extraordinary race in which there were two first-corner shunts, in the original start and on the restart. Had his brakes not begun to fade, Rubens believed he could have challenged Eddie Irvine for third place,

Suddenly, the alliance between Stewart and the Blue Oval had come under serious pressure. (Sutton)

while Jan was delighted with his first-ever World Championship point after narrowly holding off Shinji Nakano's Minardi. Sadly, the performance came too late to save his place in the team, and after Canada the Dane was replaced by Dutchman Jos Verstappen, who had been on the Stewarts' original driver short-list.

Nobody could foresee it at the time, but the team had scored its last points of the season.

Once again the French and British races brought nothing, but after the weather affected qualifying in Austria Rubens started fifth and was sitting it out with Michael Schumacher's Ferrari in a fight over fourth place when a brake problem sent him to the pits.

The remainder of the year was a blur of poor performance, gearbox failures

and disillusionment, peppered by the off-track politics. In the wake of Ford's dwindling patience the rumours grew stronger that the company was being wooed heavily by Benetton. Whitaker was known to have had several meetings with Benetton chief David Richards, to whose Prodrive company Whitaker would award the contract for 1999 to develop the Blue Oval's British Touring Car Championship programme.

At the same time, and potentially even more worrying, were events within the motor industry itself, for the Volkswagen Audi Group was moving ever closer to a deal to buy Rolls-Royce, which included Cosworth Engineering and Cosworth Racing. Ford began making contingency plans to build its own engine in-house if necessary.

A test of a solid relationship: despite the problems, Barrichello could still make Paul Stewart laugh. (Formula One Pictures)

Meanwhile, Stewart GP came in for criticism for building something as complicated as a carbon gearbox in only its second year, at a time when Ferrari had struggled unsuccessfully with the technology. Paul, however, was quick to defend the decision. 'It was a combination of wanting to take the risk with an unknown piece of technology, but one that we had the resources to develop provided that it went straight on to the car at the start of the season; and being willing to take that risk. And the other side is a little bit of naïveté as well. I still don't think it was the wrong thing to have done. Ultimately we have set ourselves a long-term plan, and those sort of things are things that we are going to have to do as a racing team in years three, four and five.'

It was unnecessarily complex technology at a time when the team had much progress to make elsewhere. But Paul further qualified the decision by adding, 'If we had tried to do it as a development project on the side, during the course of this year, I don't believe we would have had the structure and procedures to push it through. There is tremendous pressure when it's got to go on the first car – you end up doing the all-nighters, you worry about it more, you discuss more how you are going to solve the problems, and that puts a wholly different perspective on it. With the completely new regulations, we knew it was going to be difficult in the first part of the season, because we haven't got the level of sophistication in terms of analysis and procedures that other,

Ringing
the changes

At the end of the 1998 season Stewart Grand Prix made some fundamental changes to its personnel line-up. Foremost among these was the appointment of David Ring as Managing Director.

Gary Anderson journeyed to Japan with Stewart GP, having joined as chief designer. Within weeks he had settled in fully, and would soon become technical director when Alan Jenkins quit.
(Formula One Pictures)

Ring, 36, had extensive experience working in the aerospace industry, where for the past four years he had held a similar position within the Hamble Group. 'To be associated with such a high technology activity is going to be enormously exciting,' he said. 'My background is in the aerospace field which, of course, has many similarities with the world of modern Formula 1.'

Jackie Stewart expressed himself delighted to strengthen the team with such a high-calibre businessman, and both he and Paul were at pains to stress that it was not demotion for the latter, who became Deputy Chairman to his father. Instead, Paul would work more closely with Jackie on the acquisition front.

'Until you live through the tensions and the pressures of a season like 1998 you don't fully appreciate what those teams who have been in Formula 1 for a lot longer than us have had to endure,' Paul said. 'It certainly was not a comfortable position to be in, but what it has meant is that we have had to react to ensure that we are in much better shape for 1999. We have invested heavily and made changes on the engineering and manufacturing side of the operation and the overall structure of the company is much more sound.

'Invariably we have had to cope with the difficulties inherent in a natural process of accelerated growth at SGP. We now have more than 200 people working here, for example. The changes we have made will allow us to become a much more cohesive operation in 1999 and enable us to take decisions in areas of engineering much more quickly.'

At the same time, Gary Anderson had come on board as chief designer, initially to work alongside technical director Jenkins. Anderson had tired of the political struggle within Jordan, and after deciding against an initial inclination to become technical director at TWR Arrows, he joined Stewart GP in time to attend the Japanese GP, which wound up the 1998 season.

'We are excited by Gary's arrival,' said Jackie. 'He brings a wealth of expertise and has worked on many successful cars. He is a current man, and we think that in him we have someone very important.'

Before long, however, it became clear that Jenkins would not be staying, and by the start of the new season Anderson had become technical director as well. Jenkins's legacy was the Stewart SF-3, the best car the team had ever designed and built. Now it would be Anderson's responsibility to develop it.

When Ford had purchased Cosworth Racing, Stewart had also taken the opportunity to appoint Neil Ressler, who was due to take over as Vice President and Chief Technical Officer, Research and Vehicle Technology for Ford Motor Company on 1 January 1999, as a non-executive director of Stewart GP.

Ressler was Jackie Stewart's age and had a wealth of experience with Ford, having joined the company as a senior research scientist in 1967 and worked his way up to the position of Vice President, Advanced Vehicle Technology, Ford Automotive Operations in 1994. And he was, of course, the man who had first sought Jackie's advice back in 1995.

more established, teams have. So invariably there were things that potentially we were going to lose out on. But you are always hopeful, you don't go in there thinking, "We are going to throw away the first four races."'

But to an extent, that was just what had happened. Paul was happier when Rubens finished fifth in Spain, but remained cautious. 'It was a risk that I thought was worth taking, and I still don't know if it was wrong. Spain suggested it was the right thing to do! That was an important weekend for us.'

The problem was, as ever, massaging sufficient reliability into the unit, and here Stewart GP betrayed its youth. 'There are many issues,' Paul explained, 'such as the different rates of expansion of different metals and carbon fibre, which led to oil leaks. By the end of the season we were well on our way to solving them.'

He denied that the ambitious programme detracted from Alan Jenkins's other work as technical director. 'We did the gearbox in-house, in collaboration with Xtrac, and our man in charge, the gearbox designer, was Rob Dornay who worked extremely hard on it. He was responsible for it all, so it hasn't affected Alan.'

The continuing seasonal post-mortem revealed that no single problem had left one of the year's most attractive cars with fewer points than its predecessor, but several. 'Everyone says the second year is the worst, and I'm beginning to understand that,' Paul admitted. 'I didn't understand it last year, because I was thinking, "Hey, look at the things we did to get the team up and running, then racing and staying on top of our reliability problems, how can it be more difficult? The second year must be easier than this!" But what you forget, what I forgot as a manager, was that during this time last year I wasn't able to bring to the fore issues, or make decisions, that were going to be affecting us now. But now as an organisation we are far more geared up, and the team has got together more, so that this time next year, in theory, it will be much better. I'm already asking now what our plan is for this, when are we going to start that, why aren't drawings ready for this? All those sort of things that, quite frankly, when you are setting up a new organisation, pass under your nose. It's not through lack of commitment or stupidity, but you are learning the whole world of F1. It's a bit like driving into a snowstorm; you've got a huge amount of confusing data coming at you, and you have to deal with that while still remembering the basics of driving. Gradually you learn how to place things.'

It proved too big a mouthful for a small team to digest

He was, he said, also learning better how to pace himself during qualifying, to understand what was happening to each car, and what their problems were, then to have a conversation with people back at base to discuss what changes might need to be made. And 10 minutes later, being able to have a completely different meeting talking about other matters, such as the Concorde Agreement.

Like Jackie, Paul was unsettled about the talk of sharing engine supply and technology with Benetton. The five-year deal with Ford was solid, but any sharing would, in their opinion, merely weaken their own challenge.

'We have not been approached by Ford on that, and have been assured that our commitment will be honoured and that there will be no deviation from that,' Paul stressed. 'There has been no such discussion with us.

'Yes, there has been pressure from Ford, and you can't complain about that. My father and I are racers, and we want this team to win. And we're not going to get there just by being jolly about it. I might still be naive about certain things, and I might say the wrong things at times, but that's the only way I'm going to learn.'

There was even a suggestion that parties within Ford – possibly Martin Whitaker – had been taking the soundings from Benetton on an unofficial – and by inference, unapproved – basis. Again, Paul trod warily. 'I can only comment on what we have seen, and nobody has approached us one way or another. I hope that on the Stewart GP side we have been making every effort to behave in a team-like fashion on this, and in a company as large as Ford some people could be excused for saying, "What are we doing here?", when we are going through a difficult patch. That I understand.

'But from our side, when things

Team helmets, Monaco 1998. (Formula One Pictures)

Friends in high places: Jackie escorts Princess Anne in Austria, where she encountered a little more horsepower than she is used to. (Formula One Pictures)

weren't quite right on the engine side, we toed the line. It can be discouraging when you hear things, whether they are true or not, when you are giving your absolute maximum to it. The suggestions are that we are not all working together as a team. I think that's a normal insecurity that you get, but the people who are working closely on the programme have given me and my father assurances that we are all working together on this.'

By the end of the year there was a light on the horizon

All season Cosworth had kept throwing up modified versions of the Zetec R V10, running in P-coded specifications. By the end of the season there was a significant improvement, as Paul was the first to agree. 'We were able to rev better and the driveability was better. The drivers weren't complaining about the power, and each new engine was a step forward. We sat tight and waited for each one, and it allowed us to gear the cars better, which in turn also made the handling better.'

The fact remained, however, that reliability was nightmarish. Barrichello was only 12th in the drivers' championship, with Magnussen joint 15th. In the constructors', Stewart-Ford finished one place higher than in 1997, with one point fewer. Everyone had known that the second season would be tougher than the first, but nobody

had expected it to be so gruelling. A serious rethink was long overdue.

The lateness of the SF-2 and the belt-driven version of the Zetec-R V10 really hurt the team, and put it on its back foot from the word go. It was just too young to recover fully. The situation was unavoidable, given the structure and manpower of what was still a team learning the ropes at the highest level. The change to grooved tyres didn't help either. The team was obliged to play a game of catch-up all year, and also paid the price for the adventure into carbon fibre transmission casings. Though many of its problems lay in the software, rather than the casing material, it proved just too big a mouthful for a small team to chew and digest. Overall, the massive disappointment could have toppled a team that had a weaker infrastructure.

There were some good pointers to the future, however. Though Verstappen proved little quicker than Magnussen, he did help the team to regroup from mid-season onwards by exhibiting a clearer grasp of the situation and its requirements. Rubens, meanwhile, upon learning that Frank Williams was not interested in paying to buy out the remainder of his Stewart contract, stopped looking at what at the time seemed greener grass, and settled down again into his habitual role of morale booster. That was a huge relief for a team that had been built around a driver that everyone within it rated highly.

By Magny-Cours in mid-season, Jos Verstappen had replaced Jan Magnussen. (Formula One Pictures)

Good news and bad at the Nurburgring for the GP of Luxembourg: the cars were reliable enough to finish, but Rubens (above) was only 11th, Jos (below) 13th. (Formula One Pictures)

Also on the positive side, which all too often the detractors chose to ignore, the new factory was delivered on time, as promised in the original agreement with Ford. The test team was also operational by mid-season.

'All these things needed to be moving at the same time, and that required a level of understanding that you can't just develop,' Paul said. 'Of course that could be foreseen. I'm not suggesting that we were ignorant of things we had to consider during year two, because we had to plan for a factory move. That required a commitment from the Board; "Right, we are going to do this." It wasn't as if we were just looking around, and then forgot about it. We were moving forward. We were 10 years in our old 15,000 square feet base, where we had taken units on short leases, and we were looking at an 80,000 square foot unit with a 16-year lease. We really had to commit financially to that. Then there was all the machinery to go into it. Those sort of things take time.'

The construction of the Stewart Building, close to the old premises in Milton Keynes, was one of the high points of 1998. Slowly, and though it might not have seemed like it at the time, Stewart GP was making progress.

The move, of course, was disruptive, and Paul concedes that it may have played a part in the team's disappointing on-track performance. 'But I think we've done a bloody good job and it was one we had to do. If we hadn't committed when we did, we would have been looking to move right in the heart of the racing season. And the problem there is that you come back from a weekend like we had in Imola, and there is a temptation to say, "I don't want to talk about a new factory right now, I wanna talk about how we are going to fix this car."'

They might not have delivered yet on track performance, but the Stewarts had completed an important part of their original Ford proposal. 'That has been our constitution,' Paul said. 'It's not so much what do we do now, as what did we say we were going to do in our proposal? Right, we'd better do that! And we've stuck by that.

'It's not sales pitch to say that when we did the deal with Ford, we wanted a long-term trustworthy partner for Ford Motor Company to work with. That has always been a vitally important element.'

By the end of the year there was bright light on the horizon. After a period of uncertainty the Volkswagen Audi Group deal with Rolls-Royce had indeed gone ahead in September, but VAG had agreed to sell Cosworth Racing back to Ford. Ford, of course, owned the intellectual rights to the Zetec R V10, so could have continued with it even if the VAG sell-back had not gone ahead, but in motorsport circles the idea of Ford without Cosworth was like Marks without

'Happiness is ... Rubens and Sylvana Barrichello, clearly devoted to each other. (Formula One Pictures)

Spencer. It was simply unthinkable. The corollary of this good piece of news was that Ford now had a complete say in the staffing at Cosworth, and its policies.

In early November Neil Ressler, Vice President and Chief Technical Officer of Research and Vehicle Technology for Ford, was appointed Chairman of Cosworth Racing. Dick Scammell MBE, who had been acting as interim MD, would work with him to oversee the transition of Cosworth Racing into its new position as a fully owned Ford subsidiary.

Almost overnight it was as if people such as F1 project leader Nick Hayes had been liberated, for now he had absolute freedom to pursue his own avenues of development. Fortunately, he had been doing this for much of 1997, and when the fruits of his labours were finally revealed publicly in January 1999, Stewart-Ford's credibility suddenly took a massive leap forward.

At the same time, ideas of a Benetton safety net finally faded away, and Ford underlined that by agreeing a sixth year for the Stewart partnership. 'We always knew that we had our five-year programme with Ford, and that we had no intention of trying to change that,' Jackie said. 'Now I am delighted that we have signed an extension. We are very happy about Ford's commitment.'

On the driver front, Jan Verstappen's brief tenure was over. Part of the Dutchman's annoyance with the team was to learn that he was being replaced by Johnny Herbert. The double-Grand-Prix-winner was being brought in to 'strengthen the team,' Jackie said. 'Johnny has all the speed and experience to help the team take another step forward.'

Chapter 6

Running hot

Jackie and Paul Stewart could not believe their eyes. The two Stewart-Fords of Rubens Barrichello and Johnny Herbert were fourth and 11th respectively on the grid for the 1999 Australian GP, and no sooner had it dawned that one was smoking than the other also burst into flames. After all the winter hopes, and the blood, sweat and tears that had taken the team this far in its F1 campaign, it seemed a quite astonishingly cruel stroke of fortune.

What made it so much worse was the promise that the new Stewart-Ford SF-3 and its jewel of a Ford V10 engine had displayed, both in winter testing and in practice and qualifying in Melbourne.

This time there had been no disguising the underlying enthusiasm as the new car was unveiled at the Autosports Show in Birmingham in January. 'We have done everything in our power to be as well prepared for the 1999 season as we possibly can be,' Jackie said. 'The

fact that the SF-3 turned a wheel as early as December 23rd last year is testament to that. The car we ran for that shakedown was completely new – a new chassis and a brand new engine. We are further ahead with the development of SF-3 than we could possibly have forecast six months ago and I believe we are further advanced for the 1999 season than any of our competitors.'

Allowing himself a moment of reflection he summarised 1998. 'I think it's fair to say that we failed to be as competitive as I think we could have been in the latter part of year two, but the lessons of 1998 have been heeded. What has to be remembered is that we are still only in our third year of competition and we have achieved an awful lot in that short space of time. We have probably achieved more than any other modern Formula 1 team particularly when you consider we started from scratch.

'We made a commitment that the

team would not allow itself to get into the position we were in for the first race of the 1998 season in Melbourne, where we were ill-prepared. I said at the time that I will never let that happen again and I made a personal pledge to our team personnel who had worked hideous hours prior to that race that it wouldn't.

'We have a brand new Ford Cosworth engine for 1999, which is smaller, lighter and has a lower centre of gravity. A lot of what we have learned in our first two years has gone into this new car and I'm confident it will serve us well.'

He also outlined just why it is crucial for F1 teams today to have official alliances with engine manufacturers. 'Ford Motor Company's continued commitment to the Stewart-Ford alliance is extremely important to the future success of the team. In Formula 1 currently, and more particularly in the future, there has to be a major car manufacturer partnering a successful Grand Prix operation. Gone are the days when an independent team can go out and get a customer engine and go racing. They are the yesteryears. What you need today is a major manufacturer who is totally committed to being

Up in smoke: at the start of the 1999 Australian GP in Melbourne, smoke is already evident around the back of Herbert's Stewart-Ford. (Formula One Pictures)

extremely competitive and desperately wants to win Grand Prix races, win the World Championship and be recognised as the best. In the Ford Motor Company, we firmly believe we have the best.'

He said that he felt confident about the year ahead, spoke of his belief that the team was on the threshold of delivering success on a regular basis, and reiterated his optimism that in 1999 all the hard work and consequence of the harsh lessons of 1998 would bear fruit. He also said something else.

'With this car I believe that, if circumstances are favourable to us, we could win a race. We would need luck, but I believe we could do it in the right circumstances.'

It was the sort of thing that team owners are habitually wont to say on such occasions, but it was out of character for Stewart. It was as if he knew something few others in the room did. And with only marginally better fortune, he might well have been proved correct in that opening race in Melbourne.

The departed Alan Jenkins's legacy to Stewart, the SF-3, was an elegant little machine that drew heavily on McLaren's sharp-chined aerodynamic profile of 1998. Once again every aspect of the mechanical and aerodynamic package had gone back under the microscope, and wherever advantage could be taken of the small size of the Ford-Cosworth V10 CR-1 engine,

MELBOURNE MEL

The launch of the new car had been a decidedly upbeat affair, mirroring the new-found confidence in both the SF-3 and its remarkably small Ford-Cosworth CR-1 V10. (Sutton)

Jackie in Melbourne, where his belief that the right circumstances could see a victory for the team was so nearly justified first time out. (Formula One Pictures)

it had been. SGP's enhanced Design and R&D capability had helped in getting the car ready so early in comparison with the SF-2, a crucial point as new FIA technical regulations imposed a reduction on testing.

The short overall length of the CR-1 allowed greater scope in terms of positioning major components for optimum weight distribution. It had been possible to lower the centre of gravity of the car considerably, again helped by the low crankshaft height and also by a concerted design effort to place components in favourable positions. It had also been possible to lower the front of the chassis dramatically and the position of the driver's torso by more than an inch. This in turn necessitated a complete revision of the spring/damper/steering assemblies, which in any case had come under scrutiny to optimise them for the new four-groove front tyres that superseded

Multum in parvo

When Stewart-Ford launched its 1999 campaign publicly, at the Autosports Show, an unusual lump of metal was an attention-grabbing centrepiece. 'Try lifting it up,' exhorted F1 Programme Director Nick Hayes, before informing aspirant Charles Atlases that the handbag-shaped cylinder of aluminium represented the weight he had taken out of his all-new Ford V10 engine. So new was it that the Zetec-R designation had been dropped. The revolutionary power unit, thought to be the smallest in F1 history, was now called the Ford Cosworth V10 CR-1.

It measured less than 2 feet long, a fraction over 1½ wide and just over a foot high without its airbox. This little jewel weighed in at an astonishingly low 220lbs (100kg). Lower, lighter and smaller than virtually anything else on the grid, it had no carry-over parts from its predecessor and contained more innovative and radical design than ever before seen from Cosworth. Hayes had deliberately incorporated as many mountings and drives as possible for the myriad pumps and hydraulic systems, and used a brand new state-of-the-art Visteon engine management system as part of a totally integrated Vehicle Control System.

His new baby first ran on the dynamometer on 18 December 1998, and was installed in a Stewart-Ford SF3 less than a week later for its first trial runs at Silverstone. By the time rivals had had a chance to assess it on the track during its first run in anger in Barcelona, they had convinced themselves that its horsepower put it very close to the hallowed territory of Mercedes-Benz and Ferrari, and ahead of Mugen-Honda, Peugeot, Supertec and Arrows Hart.

At last, within mere months of Ford taking control of Cosworth, here was the first tangible evidence that the new philosophy formulated back in 1995 was beginning to bear fruit.

Spot the engine. Cosworth's CR-1 was small enough, but the team went to great pains to keep it concealed whenever the cars were in the pits. This is Herbert at Monaco. (Formula One Pictures)

Both Herbert (pictured) and Barrichello were on the pace throughout the weekend Down Under. (Formula One Pictures)

the three-groove rubber used in 1998. This time all of the front suspension has been produced 'in-house' from composite materials. The troublesome composite gearbox had been deleted in favour of a magnesium casing.

As the SGP Design and Manufacturing staff had grown and gained collective experience, Jenkins and his team had been able to concentrate much more on structural issues, in particular the stiffness of chassis, gearbox and suspension assemblies. This was part of an ongoing programme aided by the input from resident engineers from the Ford Motor Company.

It would later prompt the topical quote from Jackie: 'The chassis of our car is so stiff we call it the Viagra of F1!'

One area for which Jenkins had particular hope via Ford Technical Support was Vehicle Dynamics. Using Adams software and other proprietary analysis tools they had been working steadily towards a much better understanding of overall suspension characteristics and maximising the performance of the tyres.

Another area that promised extensive development potential was Visteon's VCS electronics package, a 'one box' system that catered for

'I could have won!' Barrichello didn't know whether to laugh or cry after finishing a fighting fifth, his delight in the car undermined only by the need to start from the pit lane. (Formula One Pictures)

engine management, chassis control and data logging. This state-of-the-art system would allow a development programme to proceed throughout the season, something that had been very difficult to achieve in previous years.

The stated objective for year three was to get in amongst the top four or five teams in 1999 and qualifying in Melbourne showed that the team had achieved precisely that. Then came the smoke.

'When I saw the cars smouldering on the grid, Johnny's first and then Rubens's, I just couldn't believe it,' Jackie admitted. 'I just thought, "Aw, God!" It was a situation we'd never experienced in testing.' The problem was that the cars had never been at standstill long enough with their engines idling. As the drivers waited for the red start lights to go out, small oil leaks developed that were soon ignited by the hot exhausts.

Rubens and Johnny had raved about the SF-3 from the first moment they drove it, even though a rear wing failure on the latter's car had pitched him into the wall at maximum speed down the straight at Barcelona during testing. Damon Hill described it as the worst shunt he had ever seen, but

Johnny stepped out calmly complaining of nothing worse than a stiff neck and a bruised knee.

Now Melbourne had proved them right as the SF-3s ran regularly in the top five, but while Barrichello qualified an excellent fourth on the grid, a damper problem spoiled Herbert's afternoon. He was disappointed, but the SF-3's performance was certainly no flash in the pan. 'The car should be good for the year – it has the potential if we keep developing it and exploiting the opportunities to make it better. We're not a long way back and gradually getting better, we're there or thereabouts and we can improve it more. Realistically we have a very good chance of being in the top five or six at the end of the year. It's very promising.'

Rubens agreed. He had been upbeat right from the start, speaking enthusiastically of a new start to his F1 career. 'The new car is much better than the old one in all respects,' he beamed. 'And the new Ford engine has a lot more power than last year's, for sure, especially at the top end.'

The other thing that impressed him was the team's state of preparation. 'Last year we got to Melbourne well behind schedule, and I had my car running for only five minutes of qualifying. But before Melbourne this time I tested our fourth SF-3 chassis. Jackie said last year that he would never let the team get into such a situation again, and he has been absolutely true to his word. We have never been better prepared. That gives me great confidence.'

Gary Anderson had settled in comfortably, and already it seemed as if he had been with the team since it started out on the F1 trail. 'It's nice to be where we are even if there's a lot of stuff we need to do,' he said. 'A hell of a lot has gone wrong for us, for sure, and we are confused by the damping right now, we're really not getting on top of that. It's our own system, but the concept initially was quite complex and it's been a bit of a pain. It's like anything, you've got to keep on. McLaren are obviously strong, and they're clever enough to get the car where they want it. Ferrari aren't going to be down for ever, and you'll need to be quite strong to keep up with them. But we have our own plan in place and there's quite a lot of development stuff in place.'

Herbert was unable to restart once the first start had been aborted. His car was too badly damaged. Barrichello, as faster qualifier, had rights to the spare car, which he would start from the pit lane. But he drove a storming race through the field. By the time the safety car came out after Jacques Villeneuve had crashed, he was with the leading group, but the restart frustrated his hopes. He partly overtook Mika Hakkinen's McLaren, which had been leading but which had suddenly slowed, before the start/finish line as racing resumed. It was unintentional and he had been caught out by the silver car's mechanical problems and had to accept a 10-second stop-and-go penalty. He finished fifth, disappointed but at the same time elated, as Eddie Irvine led home Heinz-Harald Frentzen and Ralf Schumacher.

'I could have won, I could have won,' he kept repeating. 'For the first time I had a car that allowed me to race and to overtake. I know that if I had started from fourth place I could have won. We had a car that could perform well, and we did that. I'm happy to finish fifth. But I'm just upset that it was a race I could have won. I tell you, it was one of the best races of my career. I was so upset, because I could have been on that podium.'

Jackie was able to offer a wry

Here's Johnny

Everybody loves his cheerful character, but by the end of 1997 few really seemed to rate Johnny Herbert any more. Jackie and Paul Stewart were not among them, however, and Herbert was clearly delighted to have signed a two-year deal to drive for them after a harrowing second season with Sauber. Ford was equally pleased to have his autograph on a contract.

Herbert looked forward to working with the Stewarts, to playing a major role within the team and its planning and development, and to having his contribution welcomed and recognised. 'I've spoken to Cosworth about changes that have been made for 1999,' he said, 'and I'm highly impressed. They've changed their way of thinking. It's not the same as it was when it was just Cosworth and the budget was set in stone. Now it seems to be completely different, and they are working the right way. That seems very good to me, one of the reasons I am very optimistic about the future. I have every faith that Stewart as a team will progress too, and I'm really optimistic. I think we have the opportunity to move ahead together.'

It was a relief for him to have sorted things out. 'It's good to know where I'm going again,' he admitted after the bruis-

If at first: Herbert tried a new helmet livery for the first four races of 1999, the green stripes matching his car's numbers. By Spain he had opted for something more patriotic. (Formula One Pictures)

ing season with Jean Alesi at Sauber. 'I can snap out of things, and push ahead again now. I feel as if I have relieved some pressure. I'm ready to fight again.'

Jackie said, 'In Rubens Barrichello and Johnny Herbert we have two well-balanced drivers who are knowledgeable, technically alert, good providers of feedback and reliable. Rubens is one of the very best drivers in the world and Johnny has the ability to motivate those around him. I think he will bring a new purpose to the team and I'm confident our two drivers will bring us the success we crave in 1999.'

'Johnny's main contribution will be in the area of experience,' Paul said. 'He is a quick driver provided we can make the conditions right for him. I think he and Rubens will motivate each other because they have complementary personalities.'

'What is so good about working with Rubens,' Johnny said, 'is that we are similar characters and believe that we should do our talking on the track. That leaves us to be friends off it.'

It took Herbert a while to get into the groove; in free practice he would be as quick as Barrichello, but in qualifying too often he seemed to overdrive the SF-3. The first five races brought the disappointment of retirement, but the breakthrough came in Canada, appropriately enough. In the race morning warm-up he tried a differential that Rubens had used all year, and which he had only just learned of, and found his car transformed. In the race he opened his points account with a stirring drive to fifth, a singularly relieved man.

He had to wait a while, but at the Nurburgring came the real reward for his loyal patience, as he became the only man to win a Grand Prix for Stewart-Ford.

Paul, Martin Whitaker, Dan Davis and Jackie finally had something to laugh about in 1999. (Formula One Pictures)

However, the smiles disappeared when Barrichello's engine broke on the 43rd lap of the Brazilian GP. (Formula One Pictures)

One race later, Rubens stormed home to third place in the San Marino GP at Imola, where he celebrated in style on the podium with winner Schumacher and runner-up Coulthard. (Formula One Pictures)

comment, to laugh at himself. 'When you're third and fifth, as we were on Friday, you start to forget the past and suddenly you're asking yourself, why can't we repeat that? Your perspective changes. But the reality of it is that the car's obviously quite good. We were disappointed the way things turned out, but to come away with fifth place ... thank you very much! We have a

Passing Damon Hill's abandoned Jordan at Monaco, Barrichello seemed headed for fifth place until the suspension broke only laps from home. (Formula One Pictures)

good package that is going to be good all season. We still have a ways to go, we know there is more to be done on the car. We know that people are going to catch up. But we know that the car has got it in it. And there is another stage on the engine to come because it's not running at full revs.

'Things are happening the right way, for the right reasons. They are very black and white. We know what we've improved, we know what we've achieved. We know the car has the right stiffness, we know all the elements of it, and that it hasn't happened by chance.'

For a while things were even more promising in Brazil. Rubens qualified third, ahead of Schumacher, then found himself in the lead after Hakkinen's McLaren suffered a momentary glitch in its gearbox on the

fourth lap. For 23 glorious laps the white and tartan Stewart-Ford led its driver's home race, and even though it did so because Stewart had opted for a two-stop race strategy compared to the single stops planned by McLaren and Ferrari, and was therefore running less fuel weight, it mattered not. It was a magnificent boost to team morale.

After the pit stops Rubens was headed for third place and a podium finish, when the engine expired on the 43rd lap. After the bottom-end had given problems in testing, then a

gudgeon pin gremlin had to be overcome, Cosworth had not been able to do a full-race testing distance at the full rev figure of 17,250rpm. In Australia, Barrichello had been limited to 16,500. 'We'll do that test this afternoon,' Hayes had smiled before the race. 'We'll just keep going until it goes bang...'

At Imola Herbert's engine, newly installed on raceday, went bang within laps of a fifth-placed finish, but Barrichello raced with 17,250rpm to take third place behind Michael

Schumacher and David Coulthard. For Stewart, it was almost as good as a win, given how competitive the car had been all afternoon.

In Monaco both cars again retired with suspension failure, Rubens in sight of fifth place, and in Spain his eighth place was taken away when the undercar plank proved to have worked loose and failed the post-race ride-height test. But this was a massive leap forward over 1998.

What was also telling was how the team sorted itself out just as it seemed to be confused during qualifying in Barcelona. 'We had a very good test here in the winter, and went well here last week,' Jackie said. 'But this weekend the weather conditions have been slightly different and that seems to have upset the fine balance of the cars. We were getting into a bit of a state on Friday, and again on Saturday morning, but I am very impressed with the way in which the team kept its head and sorted the problem out in time for qualifying. That would not have happened a year ago.' It was another sign of maturity.

Three years into its F1 programme, Stewart Grand Prix, the first F1 team ever to be founded by a former World Champion and his son, had survived the rigours of its first two seasons, and had hit back. In the Stewart-Ford SF-3 it had a car that was the envy of many of its rivals, and that would cement the foundation for the future. Now they were firmly on the right track. Then came the bombshell news in Canada:

Still in demand, thrice Monaco victor Jackie Stewart obliges autograph seekers in the Principality. (Formula One Pictures)

142

Driver, manager, owner, father: a fine balance to strike

Jackie Stewart isn't sure that being a great driver makes a great manager, though he is pretty certain that it doesn't work the other way round.

'Ken Tyrrell is a very special man. When I was racing with Ken I couldn't have asked for a better, more professional, more precise team manager, and I don't think there was another one that good when I was driving. But he wasn't a great driver! Frank Williams and Ron Dennis have had a lot of success, too, though neither of them was a particularly good driver either! I don't know whether they were frustrated race drivers who wanted to have success in racing, but they are all very focused people, that's for sure.

'I think that being a very good driver and a very good team manager may actually be mutually exclusive things. The frustrating thing is that one has to take hands off, to some extent. One cannot do everything. I learned that through Paul Stewart Racing.'

Being an owner/father isn't easy, either. 'When Paul was driving I learned to keep a distance, because I've seen so many young drivers come through PSR with fathers that were the absolute bitter end. They wanted to set the cars up, they knew better than anybody in the team. Their sons were absolutely brilliant; it was the cars' fault or the mechanics'. They wanted mechanics changed, they wanted cars changed; they threw wobblies. I could write a book on fathers!

'I was always very conscious as co-owner of the team that I could have said, "I want that for my son, and that." But I never did that. Now if I see something wrong, I want the team to know and I say it quite clearly and directly. Because I don't interfere at other times, I think they appreciate that. But if I see something wrong I'm not prepared to sit back and say it will get better if I don't touch it. That's not the way to be. The bottom line is that I'm responsible, and obviously I'm always there and available.'

Ford had purchased a 100 per cent stake in the team. Two years earlier than expected.

It had always been anticipated that Ford would take full control eventually, in line with the growing trend for car manufacturers to acquire existing specialist race teams, but most observers had expected this to occur towards the end of the five- then six-year contract. The timing took most by surprise, and only a handful of top Ford management really knew what was brewing. So what had prompted the early move?

'It has become increasingly clear to us that the way forward in Formula 1 is to maximise your firepower,' Stewart said. 'We believe that selling to Ford has enabled us to do this, and the time was right.'

Ford had been making the running, and was eager to lock itself irrevocably into a long-term motorsport programme

Rubens's efforts in securing eighth place in Spain were frustrated when he was later excluded; the undercar plank had worked loose and the Stewart failed a ride height check. (Formula One Pictures)

at a time when stability and the strength of financial and technical investment held the key to the progress that had made McLaren (with Mercedes-Benz) and Ferrari (with Fiat) so dominant.

'Formula 1 is a technical hothouse,' said Neil Ressler. 'These days a team needs vast technological and financial resources. An independent team, even like Stewart Grand Prix with Ford back-up, would be unlikely to challenge the front runners. To win the World Championship we believe it's desirable to own and run the team ourselves. It's kind of the natural next step on the longer path.

'We're doing F1 for a variety of reasons. We think it's good business to start with, and the technology and the technical training is not equalled in the world of motorsports. We will rotate our technical people through Cosworth and the F1 team. The opportunity to be seen to be operating at the highest level in a technically demanding sport was too good to miss. We are not in this just to be racing, we are in it to win.'

Ford's strategy since that cathartic meeting with Jackie Stewart, four years to the race earlier, was a clear reflection of that new philosophy. If anyone needed further proof of the new level

Johnny was also out of luck, suffering hydraulics failure. (Formula One Pictures)

Paul, Jackie and Martin Whitaker could nevertheless draw satisfaction with the way the team kept its head when struggling initially in qualifying. It was another sign of its increasing maturity. (Formula One Pictures)

of commitment to motorsport within the company, this was surely it. This was no longer mere flirting, or even cohabitation. It was marriage. At this stage the cars were expected to remain Stewart-Fords at least until the end of 1999, but the smart money was on a change of identity to Jaguar from then on.

It was a good weekend altogether for the Stewarts, as Jackie celebrated his 60th birthday – '50 and 10' as he preferred to call it. That Friday evening he dined with his family and friends at Gibby's, a fashionable eating place in old Montreal. As he walked in, fellow diners who knew him only from newsprint and television rose to sing a spontaneous verse of 'Happy Birthday'. And indeed it was. Besides

his birthday, and the sale to Ford, son Mark and his wife Anne had recently made Jackie and his wife Helen grandparents for the fourth time as Marcus came along to join Leona.

And so Ford Motor Company became the first manufacturer of the modern era to buy its specialist partner and create its own Grand Prix team, as Ferrari always has done, and as Mercedes-Benz, Honda and Renault had done with varying levels of success in the past. Ford would be represented by a small group comprising Neil Ressler, Richard Parry-Jones (Group Vice President, Product Development), Wolfgang Reitzle (Group Vice President, Premier Automotive Group) and Bob Rewey (Group Vice President of Marketing, Sales and

Services). Jackie and Paul Stewart would remain respectively as Chairman and Chief Executive Officer, and Deputy Chairman. Finely appreciative of the marketing clout of the Stewart name, there was no way that Ford was going to squander a 30-year alliance that continued to bring such strong mutual benefits.

A new chapter had begun.

Canada yielded a fifth place for Herbert and retirement through accident damage for Barrichello, but Rubens bounced back to snatch pole position in France after cannily getting out early on a wet track, in the belief that conditions would only get worse. When they did those other teams who had waited were stymied. He led the race for a while, too, and finished an excellent third. Johnny retired early with gearbox failure, and in Britain, where there was a new aero package and Michael Schumacher's shunt

Ford opens up

'This is a tough business and we would not be proceeding if our intention was not to win,' Ford Chairman and CEO Jac Nasser revealed at Hockenheim. 'Being there is not enough, but we don't have to win every time. We want to be among the winners. We do not do it for the marketing impact alone. Marketing is more impactful if you win but that is only about 20% of the reason for the programme. The other 80% is divided equally between people and technology.'

John Valentine, head of the company's Advanced Engineering racing technology division in Dearborn, Michigan, outlined further why it had been important to acquire Stewart GP, and in doing so indicated the depth of the company's previous involvement for the first time. He told Joe Saward of *F1 News:* 'We have been using our technology all along but in a very quiet way. You are seeing improvements in the car as a result of that. We were not at all pleased last year with the carbon fibre gearbox, but we did not own the team. We suggested that the carbon fibre not be used. We strongly suggested that. We strongly suggested a back-up programme – but it all fell on deaf ears. Unfortunately a lot of our suggestions were not taken and the results last year were disastrous. The fallout of that was that there was a change for this year and there is more Advanced Engineering presence in the new car.

'We have just had the Stewart-Ford SF-3 in Dearborn doing advanced analysis for the next generation car. It is like taking an F1 car to a doctor for a physical.

'When you don't own a team or an engine manufacturer you are always a little bit in an us-and-them situation. And that goes both ways because the team does not necessarily want to share everything with you. Now we can get serious. We are unencumbered in what we would like to do. It wasn't that one day we just woke up and decided what we wanted to do. It has been in the back of our minds since my group was formed in 1996. The idea was to renew our commitment to racing, increase our involvement and get the technology transfer going to help train our engineers and use racing as a test ground for new ideas and technologies.'

grabbed the headlines, both fell from sixth place. Rubens had a puncture, Johnny got a stop-and-go after fractionally nosing ahead of Alesi's stuttering Sauber before crossing the start/finish line during a restart.

In Austria there was a new electronic differential, and for the first time Herbert truly felt at one with the SF-3. He qualified sixth, right behind Rubens, but where the Brazilian fought Coulthard for the lead and ran a solid fourth before a rare engine failure, the Briton had his rear wing removed on the second corner by Mika Salo, as a corollary of the clash in which Coulthard punted off McLaren teammate Hakkinen. With a new wing fitted he fought back, to set second fastest lap.

This is the most important moment in my entire racing career

Germany brought disappointment as Rubens' hydraulics failed when he was ahead of eventual winner Irvine, while Johnny bounced back well from a dramatic rear wing failure on Saturday morning. He was winning a battle with Panis, Wurz and Coulthard for fifth place when the gearbox failed. There was another development at this point, too, for though it was not confirmed officially, the (leaping) cat was out of the bag that the Stewart-Fords would be branded as Jaguars in 2000, with Eddie Irvine partnering A.N. Other as

Rubens departed for his Ferrari seat. This was a tough period for Herbert, whose season appeared to have fallen apart again. There was much talk – plenty of it from the Stewart-Ford camp itself – of him being replaced, which seemed rich given that the car usually let him down.

Rubens was in the points again in Hungary, with fifth place, but Johnny struggled home 11th with erratic handling. Both cars lacked grip and pace at Spa, where Rubens was only 10th and a wheel bearing seizure led to brake failure and a shunt for Johnny. At Monza he made a poor start, struck the back of Panis' Prost, and lost the clutch after 41 laps. But his lap times were as fast as Rubens', who was the star as he overtook Coulthard, Salo and Zanardi en route to an excellent fourth place.

But then came the Nurburgring.

'If you go back and look at the performance of Stewart Grand Prix over the whole programme, we are ahead of where we expected to be. The aim is clearly to win and I don't think that will take long.' But when Ford Chairman and CEO Jac Nasser had uttered those words on a rare visit to Hockenheim, he had no idea how quickly he would be proved right. On the face of it, Herbert's 14th place on the grid at the Nurburgring did not auger well for the race, but what a race it turned out to be! The weather gods frowned in Germany, and the fancied runners made errors galore. Ron Dennis put Hakkinen on unsuitable wet tyres when it was good enough for dries. Coulthard threw away the lead and his championship hopes. Ferrari

Jaguar's great secret

The Stewarts were reluctant to surrender the family name on the cars they sold to Ford in June, calculating that they would be on course to win races in 2000. But Ford was adamant that it wanted the Jaguar branding by then.

'I think it is time there was more substance in Grand Prix racing,' said Jackie, who would stay on as Chairman as Paul remained Chief Operating Officer. 'Companies like Jaguar represent added value to the sport. The Jaguar name is certainly well recognised and bringing it back to motorsport at the highest level is quite important. I welcome its arrival, because it is a great added dimension. It is also important for the team that it carries on largely as it was structured in 1999, for maximum continuity. So Gary (Anderson) will be designing the new car, together with our team of engineers.'

From the outset, Jac Nasser made it clear that he saw brand loyalty for the marque's first pukka F1 effort being on a par with the tifosi's obsession with Ferrari. 'When I was in Hockenheim I saw a sea of red caps, and they made me *green* with envy...

'The important thing for us is that motorsport is an integral part of our business. It isn't different to the way we look at quality, production efficiency, marketing or finance. It has to be part of the business and therefore it has to be global and integrated with the brands that we have. Our people must absolutely feel that it's running through their bloodstream and therefore that we, as leaders of the company, are as committed to motorsport as we are to efficiency, speed, quality and product development.'

As F1's worst kept secret became official at the Frankfurt Show, Jonathan Browning, Jaguar's Managing Director, said: 'Our previous involvement in motorsport firmly convinced us that a successful racing programme brings major marketing benefits. Formula 1 is a massive global sport watched by millions of motoring enthusiasts at the race circuits and on television. It can be a valuable showcase for Jaguar technology as we expand our product range.'

At the same time Jaguar Racing confirmed, finally, that Johnny Herbert would be staying, and that as Rubens Barrichello headed for Ferrari, Johnny would be partnered by Eddie Irvine.

British Racing Green (albeit a metallic shade) made a return when Jaguar showed its prototype 2000 colour scheme at the Frankfurt Show. (LAT)

lost one of Irvine's wheels in a catastrophic pit stop. Frentzen's Jordan suffered electrical failure, then Fisichella threw away the lead for Benetton, and Ralf Schumacher got a puncture. Through it all, Johnny drove brilliantly and judged things to perfection as he swept home a lucky but deserved winner. To make it a wonderful day for Stewart-Ford, Rubens was third, right on the heels of Jarno Trulli.

This time there were none of the tears that Jackie and Paul Stewart shed at Monaco back in 1997, but the 60-year-old former triple World Champion was ecstatic to see the car bearing his name cross the finishing line first in Germany.

'This is undoubtedly the most important moment in my racing career,' he said. 'I have won Grands Prix, I have won World Championships, but to win as a Constructor is the highest emotion imaginable. I am just so delighted that we were able to do it in our own livery. That means so much to Paul and I. I am so proud of the whole team.'

The last time he had stood on the top spot of a rostrum was in Germany back in 1973, when he won his last Grand Prix. 'And you know what?' he beamed. 'The guy who flagged me off then was the same guy who flagged Johnny off this afternoon. Can you believe that? And he gave me the flag!'

As he wiped champagne out of his eyes, Stewart explained the lack of

I'm The Man! Johnny Herbert takes the first and last victory for the Stewart Grand Prix team in F1. (Formula One Pictures)

tears. 'I still don't understand what happened at Monaco, but this time it was more like being a driver, being up on the podium like that. I was thinking the way I thought when I was driving. This time I just took it all in. I was soaked in champagne, but it was worth it!'

For Herbert the victory was a timely reminder of his underrated ability, and a payback for all the aggravation that he had had to endure in a tough season. 'I have to admit it's still difficult to take it all in,' he said. 'It was a surprise, but a really nice one.' And as he recalled the defining moment, he pinpointed his first pit stop. 'We had decided to run the harder Bridgestones because the car felt better on them, and we made our stop at precisely the right time. I was thinking of Donington in 1993, and trying to read the clouds not just the weather we were getting at any one moment. When it first rained on lap 18 I was a bit surprised when people started pitting, because the track was really only damp. I stayed out. Later I went past the pits and came down to the left/right section, and it was absolutely pouring down. I looked at the clouds, and they were like a great big teardrop. The teardrop's tail was right in the middle of the scoreboard down there. I knew it wasn't going to move, because the wind had been blowing up the

The last time Jackie Stewart topped a podium was in Germany in 1973, his final championship year. Winner Johnny Herbert, JYS and Rubens Barichello after the Englishman's historic triumph (Formula One Pictures)

straight all day. So when I came in I called for wets even though they had dries ready, and in retrospect it was precisely the right thing to do. It was a bit of a risk, but it paid off.

'I was smirking a bit over the last few laps, savouring the moment, because this one was so much better than either of the other two wins. There was a lot more emotion, especially from senior people in the team. It's great for Stewart-Ford. It's Jackie's last year with the team running in his name, before the change to Jaguar, and it was wonderful to help him and Paul realise something so dear to their hearts.

'I had this silly thing I'd been saying to my crew, and on the last corner I shouted it over the radio: 'I'm The Man. I'm The Man!'

'As far as the future is concerned, I think I've been able at last to prove a point to the team, and to lay a strong claim to a successful season next year. It's the perfect way to move out of a difficult year and on to what I am sure is going to be a much better one.'

The very next race proved his ability once again, as he qualified fifth just ahead of Rubens in Malaysia, and then came close to 'winning' what turned out to be a hugely controversial race. Again opting for a one-stop strategy he stayed close to two-stopping Barrichello, and was running third behind the victorious Ferraris with three laps to run. But right behind him was late-stopping Mika Hakkinen, who had fresh tyres and a champi-

onship to win. When Johnny slid wide on his worn Bridgstones Mika was through, but without the need to conserve fuel and change up early because of the SF-3's Achilles Heel, its marginal fuel capacity, Johnny could have stayed third and been elevated to first when the Ferraris were slung out.

The Ferraris were reinstated on appeal, which set the scene for the final showdown in Suzuka. As Mika Hakkinen won his second World Championship, Johnny and Rubens struggled with less grip than they had enjoyed in Malaysia. A fumbled pit stop, in which Johnny's tyres weren't ready, dropped him from sixth to seventh, where he finished just ahead of Rubens. It was relatively disappointing, but nothing could detract from what Stewart-Ford had achieved in its short lifetime. To push Williams down to fifth place in the Constructors' Championship was highly impressive.

The cars were still close to the front, and they had still won a Grand Prix in only their third season. 'You know,' Jackie had beamed in Germany, 'it's only two years and six months since we began racing, and here we are, winning!'

By any standard, that was heady progress, and to come so close again in Malaysia was a fitting way to bring down the curtain on the tartan racers, and the F1 career of the venerable Ford logo, and to set the new stage for Jaguar.

Appendix 1

Jackie Stewart – principal successes

1964
British F3 Champion

11 victories

1965 BRM
3rd in World Championship

South African GP, East London	6
Monaco GP, Monte Carlo	3
Belgian GP, Spa-Francorchamps	2
French GP, Clermont-Ferrand	2
British GP, Silverstone	5
Dutch GP, Zandvoort	2
Italian GP, Monza	1

1966 BRM
7th in World Championship

Monaco GP, Monte Carlo	1
Dutch GP, Zandvoort	4
German GP, Nurburgring	5

1967 BRM
9th in World Championship

Belgian GP, Spa-Francorchamps	2
French GP, Le Mans	3

1968 Matra-Ford
2nd in World Championship

Belgian GP, Spa-Francorchamps	4
Dutch GP, Zandvoort	1
French GP, Rouen	3
British GP, Brands Hatch	6
German GP, Nurburgring	1
Canadian GP, Mont-Tremblant	6
USA GP, Watkins Glen	1

1969 Matra-Ford
World Champion

South African GP, Kyalami	1
Spanish GP, Montjuich	1
Dutch GP, Zandvoort	1
French GP, Clermont-Ferrand	1
British GP, Silverstone	1
German GP, Nurburgring	2
Italian GP, Monza	1
Mexican GP, Mexico City	4

1970 March-Ford, Tyrrell-Ford
5th= in World Championship

South African GP, Kyalami	3

Spanish GP, Jarama	1
Dutch GP, Zandvoort	2
Italian GP, Monza	2

1971 Tyrrell-Ford
World Champion

South African GP, Kyalami	2
Monaco GP, Monte Carlo	1
French GP, Paul Ricard	1
British GP, Silverstone	1
German GP, Nurburgring	1
Canadian GP, Mosport	1

1972 Tyrrell-Ford
2nd in World Championship

Argentine GP, Buenos Aires	1
Monaco GP, Monte Carlo	4
French GP, Clermont-Ferrand	1
British GP, Brands Hatch	2
Canadian GP, Mosport	1
USA GP, Watkins Glen	1

1973 Tyrrell-Ford
World Champion

Argentine GP, Buenos Aires	3

Brazilian GP, Interlagos	2
South African GP, Kyalami	1
Belgian GP, Zolder	1
Monaco GP, Monte Carlo	1
Swedish GP, Anderstorp	5
French GP, Paul Ricard	4
Dutch GP, Zandvoort	1
German GP, Nurburgring	1
Austrian GP, Osterreichring	2
Italian GP, Monza	4
Canadian GP, Mosport	5

The record
99 Grands Prix starts
27 victories (a record when Stewart retired)
17 pole positions
14 fastest laps
5 non-Championship F1 victories
12 F2 victories
2 Can-Am victories
1 USAC victory
6 World Sportscar victories
6 Tasman series victories (Champion in 1966)

Appendix 2

Paul Stewart Racing – principal successes

F3

1989
British F3 Championship

Snetterton, Paul Stewart   1

1990
British F3 Championship

Silverstone, Paul Stewart   4
Donington, Paul Stewart   4
Oulton park, Paul Stewart   4
Silverstone, Paul Stewart   3
Thruxton, Paul Stewart   3

1991
British F3 Championship
David Coulthard   2

Donington, David Coulthard   1
Brands Hatch, David Coulthard   1
Silverstone, David Coulthard   1
Snetterton, David Coulthard   1
Brands Hatch, David Coulthard   1
Zandvoort, David Coulthard   1

1992
British F3 Championship
Gil de Ferran   1

1993
British F3 Championship
Kelvin Burt   1

1994
British F3 Championship
Jan Magnussen   1

1995
British F3 Championship
Ralph Firman   2

1996
British F3 Championship
Ralph Firman   1

Macau F3 GP, Ralph Firman   1

1997
British F3 Championship
Johnny Kane   1

1998

British F3 Championship
Mario Haberfield   1
Luciano Burti   3

F3000

1992

Spa, David Coulthard   4
Albacete, Paul Stewart   3
Nogaro, David Coulthard   3
Magny-Cours, David Coulthard   3

1993

Pau, Paul Stewart   3

SPORTSCARS

1993

GTO class, Daytona 24 hrs
Paul Stewart   1

Appendix

Stewart Grand Prix – race by race

1997

AUSTRALIAN GP, MELBOURNE
Rubens Barrichello, retired lap 50, engine
Jan Magnussen, retired lap 37, suspension

BRAZILIAN GP, INTERLAGOS
Rubens Barrichello, retired lap 17, suspension
Jan Magnussen, dns after first start collision

ARGENTINE GP, BUENOS AIRES
Rubens Barrichello, retired lap 25, hydraulics
Jan Magnussen, retired lap 67, engine, 10th but
   not classified

SAN MARINO GP, IMOLA
Rubens Barrichello, retired lap 33, engine
Jan Magnussen, retired lap 3, spin

MONACO GP, MONTE CARLO
Rubens Barrichello, 2nd
Jan Magnussen, 7th

SPANISH GP, BARCELONA
Rubens Barrichello, retired lap 38, engine
Jan Magnussen, 13th

CANADIAN GP, MONTREAL
Rubens Barrichello, retired lap 34, gearbox
Jan Magnussen, retired lap 1, collision

FRENCH GP, MAGNY-COURS
Rubens Barrichello, retired lap 37, engine
Jan Magnussen, retired lap 34, brakes

BRITISH GP, SILVERSTONE
Rubens Barrichello, retired lap 38, engine
Jan Magnussen, retired lap 51, engine

GERMAN GP, HOCKENHEIM
Rubens Barrichello, retired lap 34, engine
Jan Magnussen, retired lap 28, engine

HUNGARIAN GP, HUNGARORING
Rubens Barrichello, retired lap 30, engine
Jan Magnussen, retired lap 6, collision

BELGIAN GP, SPA-FRANCORCHAMPS
Rubens Barrichello, retired lap 9, spin
Jan Magnussen, 12th

ITALIAN GP, MONZA
Rubens Barrichello, 13th
Jan Magnussen, retired lap 32, transmission

AUSTRIAN GP, A1 RING
Rubens Barrichello, retired lap 65, spin
Jan Magnussen, retired lap 59, engine

GP OF LUXEMBOURG, NURBURGRING
Rubens Barrichello, retired lap 44, hydraulics
Jan Magnussen, retired lap 41, driveshaft

JAPANESE GP, SUZUKA
Rubens Barrichello, retired lap 7, spin
Jan Magnussen, retired lap 4, spin

GP OF EUROPE, JEREZ
Rubens Barrichello, retired lap 30, gearbox
Jan Magnussen, 9th

World Championship for drivers
Rubens Barrichello, 13th, 6 points
(note: Michael Schumacher excluded from
second place overall)

World Championship for constructors
Stewart-Ford, 9th, 6 points

1998

AUSTRALIAN GP, MELBOURNE
Rubens Barrichello, retired lap 1, gearbox
Jan Magnussen, retired lap 2, collision

BRAZILIAN GP, INTERLAGOS
Rubens Barrichello, retired lap 57, gearbox
Jan Magnussen, 10th

ARGENTINE GP, BUENOS AIRES
Rubens Barrichello, 10th
Jan Magnussen, retired lap 18, transmission

SAN MARINO GP, IMOLA
Rubens Barrichello, retired lap 1, collision
Jan Magnussen, retired lap 9, gearbox

SPANISH GP, BARCELONA
Rubens Barrichello, 5th
Jan Magnussen, 12th

MONACO GP, MONTE CARLO
Rubens Barrichello, retired lap 12, suspension
Jan Magnussen, retired lap 31, suspension

CANADIAN GP, MONTREAL
Rubens Barrichello, 5th
Jan Magnussen, 6th

FRENCH GP, MAGNY-COURS
Rubens Barrichello, 10th
Jos Verstappen, 12th

BRITISH GP, SILVERSTONE
Rubens Barrichello, retired lap 40, engine
Jos Verstappen, retired lap 39, engine

AUSTRIAN GP, A1 RING
Rubens Barrichello, retired lap 9, brakes
Jos Verstappen, retired lap 52, engine

GERMAN GP, HOCKENHEIM
Rubens Barrichello, retired lap 28, gearbox
Jos Verstappen, retired lap 25, transmission

HUNGARIAN GP, HUNGARORING
Rubens Barrichello, retired lap 55, gearbox
Jos Verstappen, 13th

BELGIAN GP, SPA-FRANCORCHAMPS
Rubens Barrichello, dns after initial start
  collision
Jos Verstappen, retired lap 9, engine

ITALIAN GP, MONZA
Rubens Barrichello, 10th
Jos Verstappen, retired lap 40, transmission and
  overheating

GP OF LUXEMBOURG, NURBURGRING
Rubens Barrichello, 11th
Jos Verstappen, 13th

JAPANESE GP, SUZUKA
Rubens Barrichello, retired lap 26, differential
Jos Verstappen, retired lap 2, gearbox

World Championship for drivers
Rubens Barrichello 12th, 4 points
Jan Magnussen 15th=, 1 point

World Championship for constructors
Stewart-Ford 8th, 5 points

1999

AUSTRALIAN GP, MELBOURNE
Rubens Barrichello, 5th
Johnny Herbert, DNS, caught fire on grid

BRAZILIAN GP, INTERLAGOS
Rubens Barrichello, retired lap 43, engine
Johnny Herbert, retired lap 15, hydraulics

SAN MARINO GP, IMOLA
Rubens Barrichello, 3rd
Johnny Herbert, retired lap 59, engine

MONACO GP, MONTE CARLO
Rubens Barrichello, retired lap 72,
   suspension/accident
Johnny Herbert, retired lap 33, suspension

SPANISH GP, BARCELONA
Rubens Barrichello, 8th but disqualified, plank
   infringement
Johnny Herbert, retired lap 40, hydraulics

CANADIAN GP, MONTREAL
Rubens Barrichello, retired lap 14, accident
   damage
Johnny Herbert, 5th

FRENCH GP, MAGNY-COURS
Rubens Barrichello, 3rd (pole position)
Johnny Herbert, retired lap 5, gearbox

BRITISH GP, SILVERSTONE
Rubens Barrichello, 8th
Johnny Herbert, 12th

AUSTRIAN GP, A1-RING
Rubens Barrichello, retired lap 56, engine
Johnny Herbert, 14th, four laps down (second
   fastest lap)

GERMAN GP, HOCKENHEIM
Rubens Barrichello, retired lap seven, hydraulics
Johnny Herbert, 11th but retired lap 41, gearbox

HUNGARIAN GP, HUNGARORING
Rubens Barrichello, 5th
Johnny Herbert, 11th

BELGIAN GP, SPA-FRANCORCHAMPS
Rubens Barrichello, 10th
Johnny Herbert, retired lap 28, wheel
   bearing/brake failure/accident

ITALIAN GP, MONZA
Rubens Barrichello, 4th
Johnny Herbert, retired lap 41, clutch

GP OF EUROPE, NURBURGRING
Rubens Barrichello, 3rd
Johnny Herbert, 1st

MALAYSIAN GP, SEPANG
Rubens Barrichello, 5th
Johnny Herbert, 4th

JAPANESE GP, SUZUKA
Rubens Barrichello, 8th
Johnny Herbert, 7th

World Championship for drivers
Rubens Barrichello 7th, 21 points
Johnny Herbert 8th, 15 points

World Championship for constructors
Stewart-Ford 4th, 36 points

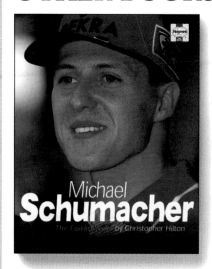
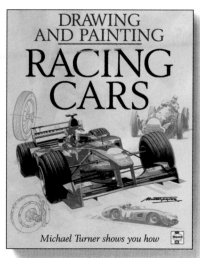
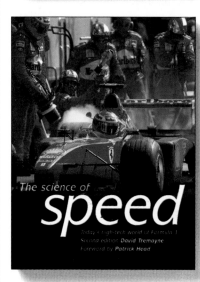
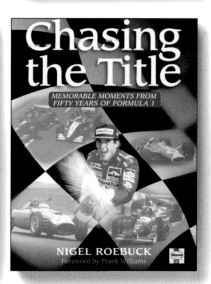
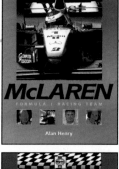

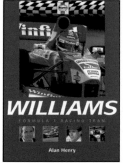